Thinking Reading Writing

Also available from Continuum

Sue Cowley: *Starting Teaching*

Robert Fisher: *Teaching Thinking*

Diane Montgomery: *Spelling*

John Wilson: *Key Issues in Education and Teaching*

Thinking Reading Writing

A Practical Guide to Paired Learning
with Peers, Parents and Volunteers

Keith Topping

With accompanying website:
www.dundee.ac.uk/psychology/TRW

CONTINUUM
London and New York

Continuum

The Tower Building
11 York Road
London SE1 7NX

370 Lexington Avenue
New York
NY 10017-6503

www.continuumbooks.com

First published 2001

British Library Cataloguing-in-Publication Data
A catalogue record for this book is available from the British Library.

ISBN 0-8264-4946-8 (hardback)
    0-8264-4945-X (paperback)

Typeset by BookEns Limited, Royston, Herts.
Printed and bound in Great Britain by Biddles Ltd, Guildford and King's Lynn

Contents

1 Introduction: How To Use This Book

What this book is about

Literacy skills are crucially important in the world of today – for progress within the education system and for coping with life outside and beyond it. However, literacy standards are not rising in line with rising expectations and demands.

Parents, peers and volunteers are increasingly involved in literacy skills tutoring – at school, in the home and in other contexts. This book extends these developments into higher order reading skills and thinking skills – currently areas of great interest to educators, government policy-makers, and employers.

The book details specific structured methods for improving quality and effectiveness in parent, peer, and volunteer tutoring. The methods cover reading, thinking, writing and spelling. They are solidly based on decades of work in hundreds of schools with thousands of children, and a mass of research evidence.

These practical methods are designed so all can benefit, tutors as well as tutees, irrespective of age and ability. They are:

- inexpensive to use
- flexible and durable in a wide range of settings
- compatible with professional instruction of almost any type
- require no special materials or complex technology.

Full descriptions of the methods are coupled with detailed advice about successful organization, brief summaries of the relevant research findings, and guidance on local evaluation. The book is linked with a website containing over 60 free resource materials to help with implementing projects and with staff development presentations; they can be adapted and copied by individual users (the *Thinking Reading Writing* TRW website – www.dundee.ac.uk/psychology/TRW).

This book and the electronic resources together are intended to make innovation and quality improvement easier, quicker and more assured for busy professionals who are striving to raise standards of achievement, improve school effectiveness, and develop collaborative community partnerships.

The methods described in this book are also enjoyable, sociable, and intrinsically rewarding. They can help to create a cooperative and positive social ethos and promote social inclusion and citizenship.

This book builds upon the author's previous book *Paired Reading, Spelling and Writing: The Handbook for Teachers and Parents* (Topping, 1995a), but substantially updates and expands it.

Who this book is for

The book is *A Practical Guide*. Although the guidance is evidence-based, the research basis for it is not given in detail. Few practitioners have time for this. More detail of this kind will be found in the many publications referred to in the text.

The book and the accompanying electronic resources will be of interest to:

- practicing teachers
- teacher educators and trainers (pre-service and in-service)
- consultants and those who advise, appraise and manage teachers, schools, and school systems
- organizers of before-school, after-school, and summer school supported study provision
- other agencies or professionals involved in the organization of parent, peer or volunteer tutoring (community educators, voluntary organizations, libraries, adult education facilities, and parents' groups)
- some parents, particularly those educating their children at home
- those interested in family literacy, workplace literacy, and other contexts for lifelong learning. (The methods have

been used successfully with adults of limited literacy as both tutees and tutors.)

- those interested in evidence-based methods for raising achievement
- those interested in evidence-based methods for promoting social inclusion and citizenship.

Recent developments

By the early 1980s, more teachers had begun to accept that parent and peer tutoring activities were 'a good thing', but many felt they were much too busy with the demands of direct classroom teaching to be able to take on this 'extra' task. Research in London caused many to change their minds (Tizard *et al.*, 1982). The impact of parental involvement in a reading project in a disadvantaged area was compared with the effect of extra small-group help from qualified reading teachers, and with regular classroom instruction alone. The parent involvement group showed far bigger gains on reading tests than the other two groups. Even more striking, the differences between the groups were still clearly evident at follow-up three years later (Hewison, 1988).

Thus it became clear to teachers that to spend a little of their precious time on organizing tutoring by non-teachers was a far more cost-effective way of managing children's learning than spending all their time on direct classroom teaching. No longer was it good enough to involve a few trusted white middle-class mothers in 'helping with reading' in school as a token gesture. The need was to involve a large cross-section of parents of all genders, races, socio-economic classes and linguistic backgrounds. If the school was able to involve grandparents, siblings, other family members, friends and neighbors, and the extended peer group as well, so much the better.

Educators from several countries increasingly sought to develop a range of effective tutoring strategies, specially designed for use by non-professionals, which could be 'given away' as part of the process of empowering the community to help itself. Such tutoring methods would not be 'watered down' versions of what teachers would do in class, but were specifically designed to capitalize on the strengths of non-professional tutors, while protecting against the impact of any weaknesses such tutors might have. The methods needed to complement, consolidate and extend regular classroom instruction rather than be considered a substitute for it. The methods presented in this book are the result of such developments.

Such tutoring systems also needed to be extremely flexible and capable of wide application. All kinds of tutoring constellations might spring up once a family had become skilled and confident in the methods. Father might tutor son who then tutored mother who then felt able to tutor younger daughter except on the hard bits where son takes over, for instance. In a family where English is an additional language, a dual language text might permit the father to tutor the son in reading the mother tongue, while the son tutored that father in reading English. This would be truly family literacy. The developing research gives encouragement that at least some family literacy programs show measurable gains in literacy skills for both tutors and tutees (Scoble *et al.*, 1988; Topping, 1995b, 1996; Topping and Wolfendale, 1995; Wolfendale and Topping, 1996).

However, developing family programs is hard work, especially the first initiative in a poor neighborhood, historically unused to such partnerships. Some professionals are easily dispirited and do not persist long enough to achieve the critical mass which makes such programs self-sustaining. Schools have many other pressures, such as testing, the prescription of a (crowded) national or mandatory curriculum, or external inspection.

At the end of the 1990s, although parental involvement figured strongly in government rhetoric, the real effect of other changes and pressures seemed to be a slowing down in work with parents – at best a plateau phenomenon. However, the pressure to 'do more with less' increased. In striving to raise attainments, some schools turned increasingly to various forms of peer tutoring in reading. It would be most unfortunate if peer tutoring were seen as a substitute for parental involvement. It is certainly potentially powerful and effective. Teachers find it attractive because it requires relatively little teacher energy to establish and is very much under the direct control of the school. Peer tutoring can also improve school ethos and relationships between children (Topping and Ehly, 1998; Topping, 2001a). However, family programs can improve relationships between adults and children throughout the local community, an important factor in an area where schools are competing for clients.

Other types of tutors have also been involved: volunteer parents in schools and neighborhoods, non-teaching staff in schools, senior citizens, students (sometimes themselves with special needs), and so on. In the US, recent legislation has promoted tutoring in literacy by a wide range of volunteer adults, including college students and America Corps recruits. These programs have been designed to focus on emergent and early novice readers as tutees, not the easiest group with which to work. Programs have varied in method, quality and degree of connection with local schools (Topping, 1998a). Recent research in the UK showed that volunteers working with emergent readers in classrooms in disadvantaged areas do not necessarily show greater measurable effects than same-school control groups, even with training and supervision (Elliott *et al.*, 2000). Additional adult support does not by itself necessarily lead to gains in children's learning. High quality methodology, planning, training, implementation and monitoring are crucial.

The methods presented in this book are evidence-based, typically yield substantial measurable benefits in relation to their low cost and incorporate their own evaluative framework. Of course, just because a method is effective does not ensure that it continues to be used. Some teachers may lose interest in a particular method because it is not 'the latest thing'. Fortunately most teachers are too sensible and pragmatic to be so easily influenced by concern with novelty. Indeed, amidst much talk of higher standards, targets, accountability and cost-effectiveness, governments world-wide are showing increased interest in evidence-based strategies and issues of school effectiveness (see, for example, Postlethwaite and Ross, 1992; Topping, 1995c; Teddlie and Reynolds, 1999). The Paired Reading, Paired Thinking, Paired Writing and Cued Spelling methods presented in this book are not the only methods you can use. However, they are among the most clearly structured and best evaluated.

The focus of this book is on literacy and thinking skills, and this is indeed an excellent place to start, but there are possibilities in other curriculum areas. A great deal of work has been done on parent and peer tutoring of mathematics and science (see, for example, the Family Math program by Stenmark *et al.*, 1986; Topping, 1998b;

Topping and Bamford, 1998a,b). As literacy is redefined in an electronic environment through links with information and communications technology, new programs are exploring 'family electronic literacy' and 'tele-tutoring' (Topping, 1997a; Topping *et al.*, 1997).

Peer assisted learning (PAL) is increasingly extended to younger tutors in equal opportunity class-wide programs, including tutors who themselves have special needs. PAL has encompassed virtually all curriculum areas, often with more complex and challenging content, and with greater focus on gains for tutors. Interest in materials-free tutoring procedures and same-ability reciprocal tutoring has grown. Tutoring has been combined with curriculum-based formative assessment. Tutoring by peers, family and volunteers continues to be an exciting growth area (Topping, 2000, 2001a, b).

International terminology

Countries organize their education systems in different ways and use different terms to describe them. Two kinds of confusion can arise: where different terms are used to mean the same thing, and where the same terms are used to mean different things. Some of the most common differences in vocabulary between the US and the UK are discussed below.

Students/Pupils

In the US and Canada, learners in all kinds of schools, colleges and universities are often called 'students'. In the UK, the term is only used for learners in colleges and universities; learners in schools are 'pupils' or 'schoolchildren'.

Grades

In the US and Canada, grades are developmental levels of competence in school roughly corresponding to chronological years, but with the implication that children should meet the minimum level of competence for one grade before proceeding to the next (although this might not be enforced in practice). Grades are also found in some countries in South America. Most of the rest of the world groups children simply by chronological year, and all children progress with advancing age. Exceptions are in small (often rural) schools and in developing countries, which may have children from several years in one class. American grade 1 (five–six-year-olds) roughly equates to English Year 1 (although in England there is a reception year and in the US and Canada one or two kindergarten years) and to Scottish P2 (Primary 2), and so on.

Types of school

In the US and Canada, elementary schools are for children aged approximately 5 to 11. These are called primary schools in the UK. Schools for children aged roughly 11 to 18 are called 'high schools' in North America, 'secondary schools' in the UK. In some parts of both North America and the UK, middle schools take children from about 9 or 10 until 12 to 13.

Special needs

Children with unusual or exceptional difficulties or needs in learning or coping with the school environment are termed children with 'special educational needs' (SEN) in the UK. In the US and Canada, the vernacular expression 'special ed. students' is sometimes heard, but is often unacceptable to the students and their families. North America has an elaborate quasi-medical typology for labeling different kinds of difficulty in children (DSM-IV). In the UK legislation largely prohibits such labeling and mandates a more specific and pragmatic focus on the special educational needs of individuals in relation to their current context.

Children from minority backgrounds in relation to the dominant local population are sometimes so identified in both the US and the UK, with the nature of the minority specified (ethnic, religious, cultural). Children whose first language at home is not English are sometimes identified as ESL (English as a Second Language) pupils or more recently ESOL (English as a Second or Other Language) and EAL (English as an Additional Language) in the US and the UK.

In relation to this, the standard or usual materials, arrangements, etc. are often called 'regular' in the US and Canada and 'ordinary' or 'normal' in the UK Educational programs which require the removal of children (in a small group or singly) from the main classroom are often called 'pull-out' programs in the US and Canada, 'withdrawal' in the UK.

Education management

In the US, education is a provincial and state responsibility, jealously guarded. Consequently, there is little national standardization of what schools have to teach, although there are some national assessments for older students. Sometimes individual states provide curriculum guidelines, more or less prescriptively, which may relate to state-wide achievement tests where these are required. Within states, individual school districts can also vary in the amount of curriculum prescription and mandated testing of outcomes. Within individual schools, the senior manager is known as the school principal.

In England and Wales, there is a prescribed and standardized 'National Curriculum' with which all publicly funded schools must comply. There are also national tests at intervals throughout a student's school career, national examinations at the end of secondary school, and a national school inspection system. Scotland and Northern Ireland have different systems. Local government is in the form of councils or local authorities, which previously used to allocate funds from central and local taxation to education. However, funds are increasingly channeled directly to schools, and the functions of local authority education departments have been reduced. Within individual schools, the senior manager is usually known as the head teacher.

Computers

In US schools, computer provision is typically relatively high, even some elementary schools having computer labs as well as many computers in classrooms. In the UK, although secondary schools may have computer labs, primary schools typically make do with one or more computers in each classroom. The UK has also been handicapped by years of dependency upon a hardware platform and operating system which was idiosyncratically British and is now obsolete. Both countries suffer from an accumulation of out-dated and ill-serviced hardware, and problems with training teachers and keeping them updated (particularly about software). UK schools have adopted the standard term 'Information and Communications Technology' (ICT) to refer to this aspect of learning (the nomenclature of the National Curriculum).

Miscellaneous

Free time between lessons is 'break' in the UK, 'recess' in the US. 'Basal readers' (US) are known as 'reading schemes' in the UK. When formally assessing work (especially written work), UK teachers 'mark' it, while US teachers 'grade' it.

How this book is organized

This book considers tutoring in Reading, Thinking, Writing and Spelling. The specific methods presented are structured Paired Reading (also known as Duolog Reading), Paired Thinking, Paired Writing and Cued Spelling. The methods are presented in this order, in four parts, after this Introduction.

Each of these parts has four chapters:

- What Is the Method? (detailed description)
- How To Organize the Method (guidance on successful planning/implementation)
- Does the Method Work? (brief summary of existing evidence of effectiveness)
- How To Evaluate the Method (ways of collecting evidence of effectiveness).

At many points throughout the text, readers are referred to relevant resources on the TRW website which accompanies the book.

Part One covers Paired Reading and is longer than the other sections. This is because most readers who are new to Paired Learning start with a Paired Reading initiative, and some of the advice on organizing Paired Reading also applies to the other areas. Reading at least the first two chapters of Part One is recommended before dipping into other parts.

Part Five includes a chapter on extending and embedding your initiative after a first successful pilot project. It also includes a complete overview of the resources which can be freely obtained from the TRW website which supports the book. A full listing of the Resources is given here under the headings:

- General Resources for Tutoring
- Paired Reading
- Paired Thinking
- Paired Writing
- Cued Spelling.

Information about other relevant resources is included.

Acknowledgements

The author acknowledges his debt to a great many professional colleagues, students, parents and volunteers whose energy, commitment and creativity over the years are reflected in these pages. However invidious, special mention must be made of Whitney Barrett, Angela Bryce, and Janie McKinstery, whose work features in Chapter 8, of which they are co-authors.

Action implications

The author and the publishers wish readers well in their efforts to put these methods into practice. With the support of the methods, guidance and resources presented here and on the TRW website, you should be much less reliant on good luck than would otherwise be the case.

Part One
Paired Reading

2 What Is Paired Reading?

The term 'Paired Reading' has such a warm, comfortable feel to it that some teachers have loosely applied it to almost anything that two people do together with a book. Of course, the effectiveness research only applies to 'proper' Paired Reading, the specific structured technique described below.

Some teachers have invented their own procedures, cheerfully (mis-)labeled them Paired Reading, then found they did not work too well, and looked around for somebody else to blame. This dilution through problems of loose nomenclature and poor implementation integrity can easily result in muddled attitudes to the technique. Indeed, in the US, the need was felt to re-label 'proper' Paired Reading to try to avoid this kind of confusion. Teachers felt the new term 'Duolog Reading', was unusual enough to remain clearly identifiable in an educational marketplace overwhelmed with a plethora of methods.

Paired Reading elements

The elements in Paired Reading are described below.

Selecting reading material
The tutees choose reading material of high interest to them from the school or community library or home. Newspapers and magazines are fine. However, if the tutee has an fanatical interest in one topic or type of book that is not shared by the tutor, some negotiation will be needed, to avoid excruciating boredom for the tutor.

Because Paired Reading is a kind of supported or assisted reading, tutees are encouraged to choose material above their independent reading level. Tutees will not benefit if they select books that are easy for them to read. Of course, the material must not be above the independent reading level of the tutor.

The pair can use the 'Five Finger Test' of readability:

- open a page at random
- spread five fingers
- place fingertips on the page at random
- tutor attempts to read the five words
- repeat on another four pages
- if tutor has struggled on more than one or two words, the book is too hard.

Tutees can do something similar to check if the book is too easy for Paired Reading (in which case they could read the book independently at another time).

If the tutees become bored with the book they have chosen and want to change it, that is OK.

Contact time

Pairs commit themselves to an initial trial period of at least fifteen minutes per day at least three times per week for eight weeks. It is best if there is consistently one main tutor to start. Later, various members of the family or even friends and neighbors can help. However, everyone must do Paired Reading in just the same way, or the child will get confused. For peer tutoring, the three sessions per week should be in regular scheduled class time, with the possibility of doing more during recess (break) if the pair wish. This frequency of usage over the initial period enables the pair to become fluent in the method and is sufficient to begin to see some change in the tutee's reading.

Place and position

Finding a relatively quiet and comfortable place is desirable, not easy in a busy school or home. Pairs should keep away from televisions or computers, and other distracting noise or activity.

It is important that both members of the pair are sitting comfortably together side by side and can see the book equally easily. In the home, Paired Reading provides an all too rare opportunity to get close to each other.

Discussion

Pairs are encouraged to talk about the book, to develop shared enthusiasm and to ensure the tutee really understands the content (without seeming like a test). Of course, discussion may be noisy.

Pairs should:

- talk about the pictures
- talk about interesting words or ideas or events
- talk at some natural break like the end of a sentence, paragraph, page or section, or the tutee may lose track
- ask what the tutee thinks might happen next
- listen to the tutee: tutors should not do all the talking
- review the main ideas or events at the end of chapters and at the end of the book.

Pointing

Tutors often ask 'Should we point at the words?' The answer is not just 'yes' or 'no'. On a hard book, or when the tutee is tired or not concentrating well, pointing may help. But tutors should only do it when necessary, not all the time. And if the tutee can do it rather than the tutor, that is preferable. Sometimes both can point together.

Correction

A very simple and ubiquitously applicable correction procedure is prescribed. When the tutee says a word wrong, the tutor just tells the tutee the correct way to say the word, has the tutee repeat it correctly, and the pair carry on. Saying 'No!' and giving phonic or any other prompts is forbidden. Tutors do not make the child struggle and struggle, 'break it up' or 'sound it out.'

There will be some words neither tutee nor tutor will know. Tutors are not expected to know everything. Tutors must not bluff. If they do not understand, they must say so to the tutee. Then the tutee can ask a teacher.

Pause

However, tutors do not jump in and pronounce the word right straight away. The rule is that tutors pause and give tutees four seconds to see if they will put it right by themselves. Tutees will not learn to self-correct if not allowed the opportunity to practice this. Holding off for four seconds is not easy. Tutors can be encouraged to count slowly to four in their heads before allowing themselves to interrupt.

The exception to this rule is with the rushed and impulsive reader. In this case earlier intervention and a finger point from the tutor to guide racing eyes back to the error word is necessary.

Praise

Praise for good reading is essential. Tutors should look pleased as well as saying a variety of positive things.

Praise is particularly required for:

- good reading of hard words
- getting all the words in a sentence right
- putting wrong words right before the tutor does (self-correction).

PR does not proscribe undesirable behaviors (since that is usually ineffective), but instead promotes effective and desirable behaviors which are incompatible with the undesirable ones.

Reading Together

How can tutees manage difficult books? Tutors support tutees through difficult text by Reading Together. Both members of the pair read all the words out loud together, with tutors modulating their speed to match that of the tutees, while providing a model of competent reading. Tutees must read every word and errors are corrected as above.

Signaling for Reading Alone

When an easier section of text is encountered, the tutee may wish to read a little without support. Tutor and tutee agree on a way for the tutee to signal for the tutor to stop Reading Together. This could be a knock, a sign, a nudge, or a squeeze. The signal must be clear, easy to do and agreed before starting. When the tutee signals, the tutor stops reading out loud right away, while praising the tutee for being so confident.

Return to Reading Together

Sooner or later while Reading Alone the tutee will make an error which they cannot self-correct within four seconds. Then the tutor applies the usual correction procedure and joins back in Reading Together.

The Paired Reading cycle

The pair go on like this, switching from Reading Together to Reading Alone, to give the tutee just as much help as is needed at any moment.

If the tutee has chosen a hard book, more Reading Together will be needed, and less Reading Alone. If the tutee has chosen a relatively easier book, less Reading Together will be needed and there will be more Reading Alone. Tutees should never 'grow out of' Reading Together – they should always be ready to use it as they move on to harder and harder books. If tutees seem to be doing a great deal of Reading Alone, it is probably a sign that the books they are choosing are too easy for Paired Reading.

Young able readers sometimes have difficulty accepting this, as they are conditioned to assume that reading independently is the 'grown-up' way to read. In fact, of course, reading independently is only one way to read books, and then only books that are within your current independent readability level. Also, no matter how good they are at the moment, everyone can always get better at reading. This should be made explicit in training sessions.

Sticking to the 'rules'

Pairs should try to make sure they stick to these 'rules', at least for the initial period. If they do not, they are likely to get in a muddle. Each member of the pair should make sure they do not do each other's 'job'. The tutee signals to silence the tutor from Reading Together – tutors cannot decide to go quiet when they feel like it. Also, when the tutee makes a mistake when Reading Alone that they do not self-correct in four seconds, the tutor must correct it and go back to Reading Together. The tutee might ask the tutor only to give them the word they got stuck on, and let them carry on Reading Alone – but that's not what the 'rules' say.

Resource materials

The resource materials on the TRW website include a specimen How To Do It leaflet for parents and a specimen How To Do It leaflet for peer tutoring. You might wish to look at those now. You will also find some overhead masters to use when presenting the method to staff development sessions or to training meetings. The PR flowchart on the TRW website gives a graphical outline of how the system operates. This is too complex to give to most tutors at the outset, however.

The need for practice

The best way to get to know Paired Reading is actually to do it. This applies to you as well as to those you may wish to tell about the method. Try to find a child who will let you practice. After this experience, this chapter and the method will make much more sense. Of course, you cannot make generalizations from a sample of one, so if you can practice on more than one child, this will be even better.

PR with non-readers

Paired Reading is designed to work with children who have already made some sort of a start with reading (typically a minimum sight vocabulary of one hundred words or so). If you wish to use the method with tutees who are in the first stages of developing literacy, some adaptations are necessary.

A great deal more discussion to support understanding is necessary. You will need to control the readability of the books from which the pair choose to a much lower level, nearer that of the tutee. If possible, you may create some personalized reading books, including details and illustrations from the tutee's life experience. Encourage repeated reading of favorite books, with the tutor reading the book to the tutee on the first occasion, Reading Together on the second, moving into full Paired Reading with increased tutee independence on each re-reading.

Other languages and restricted literacy in the home

For use with families or peer tutoring situations where the participants are bilingual, you may wish to have the leaflet for tutors translated. Examples of such translations have not been included in the Resources, because the list of possible languages would be very long, not least because local dialects are so various.

You may feel that such translated leaflets would be of little use where many of the bilingual (ESOL) population are not literate in their mother tongue. However, Paired Reading is very flexible and can be used in many ways to develop family literacy. Sometimes children will take home How To Do It leaflets in English and mother tongue, dual language books, audio-tapes of single or dual language texts. An uncle might use Paired Reading to help the child and the parents learn to read the mother tongue, while the child uses the method to teach his or her parents to read English.

If you are working with families that are monolingual in English, in which it is difficult to find any member with a literacy capability any higher than that of the target child, you may wish to consider using texts of much more controlled readability, supported by audio-tape readings (see Topping *et al.*, 1997).

How does PR work?

Of course there is relatively little new about Paired Reading. Some aspects of long-standing practice have merely been put together in a particularly successful package. However, it is this precise combination which has been proven. Remember that PR does not constitute the whole reading curriculum. It is designed to complement professional teaching but not to interfere with it.

In the US, a number of approaches showing some of the features of Paired Reading have been developed over the years. These include Reading-While-Listening, the Lap Method, Shadow Reading, Duet Reading, Assisted Reading, Prime-O-Tec, Talking Books and the more fearsomely named Neurological Impress Method. Few of these were designed for use by non-teachers, however. Nevertheless, no single feature of Paired Reading is new. The effectiveness of the technique lies in the assembly and coherence of its elements, the total engineered package. The whole is more than the sum of its parts.

The Paired Reading method has a number of advantages. Some of these are common to other methods where parents or peers help with reading, but many are specific to the Paired Reading method. When you are introducing the method to new users, some of them may ask about the reasons for the Paired Reading rules. To help you answer such questions, and for your own information, you will want to be familiar with the content of the handout The Advantages of Paired Reading on the TRW website. Regard this as an optional handout only for those who are deeply interested, otherwise you run the risk of drowning people with too much information.

The Paired Reading method obviously increases the amount of practice at reading, the importance of which has again been demonstrated (Topping and Paul, 1999). Practice consolidates a skill, promotes fluency and minimizes forgetting. Crucially, PR ensures that this practice is positive and successful. PR includes both modeling and scaffolding of correct reading, and thus provides a bridge between listening comprehension and independent reading comprehension. Good and weak readers typically differ much less in listening comprehension than they do in independent reading comprehension. Simultaneous reading and listening, as in Reading Together, is likely to free the struggling reader from a preoccupation with laborious decoding and enables other reading strategies to come into play. If the 'limited processing capacity' of the weaker reader is totally devoted to accurate word recognition or phonic analysis and synthesis, no processing capacity is left to deploy other strategies such as using contextual clues.

However, while Reading Alone, tutees are free to use whatever reading strategies they wish at any moment, strategically deploying a range of decoding or psycholinguistic strategies from word to word or sentence to sentence. They may use strategies they have been specifically taught or strategies they have developed for themselves. Nevertheless, if they cannot select and successfully apply a strategy with the speed and fluency dictated by the four second pause, the feedback and support of Reading Together switches in before the tutee becomes disconnected from the process of extracting meaning from the text.

PR provides:

- modeling
- practice that is successful with extraction of meaning

- scaffolding
- feedback
- praise and other social reinforcement
- supported opportunities to experiment with the effectiveness of a wide range of reading strategies in a wide range of applications.

PR also:

- enables tutees to pursue their own interests and motivations
- is highly adapted to the individual learner's needs of the moment
- promotes learner-managed learning and self-efficacy
- gives continuity – a 'flow experience'
- eliminates the tutee's fear of failure
- reduces the tutor's anxiety and confusion.

Many who have experienced PR liken it to how they learned to ride a bicycle. At first, learning to balance, steer and pedal simultaneously seems impossible, although each might be managed separately. However, with a parent or older sibling holding the frame and running alongside to share the balancing and steering burden, it quickly seems possible and before long is independently effortless.

Without a PR approach, there is some evidence that weak readers are likely to be interrupted more frequently and more immediately as compared to fluent readers, and are more likely to be given phonic prompts for individual words. Such 'help' actually reduces the contextual and other psycholinguistic clues available to the reader and is likely to create learned helplessness.

You may want to go on to consider in greater depth the research on why Paired Reading works. Some of this research is summarized in Chapter 4, Topping (1995a) and Topping and Lindsay (1992a,b). Paired Reading is now acknowledged to have wide ranging effects which are considered desirable by virtually all of the many different schools of thought on the teaching of reading. It is likely that different tutees benefit via different pathways or combinations of pathways. Attempts to find out which single route has the biggest effect for the largest number of children are probably only of academic interest.

A linguistic health warning

It should now be clear that Paired Reading is a specific name for a specific technique. It is not any old thing that two people feel like doing together with a book. Unfortunately the name has become too widely misused. You will often meet people who say 'Oh, yes, we do Paired Reading'. When you actually look at what they are doing you often find that it is nothing like the specific method described above. So take care – just because you use the same name as someone else, it does not mean that the same ideas or practice are necessarily attached to the label. Take time to make sure that you are actually talking the same language.

3 How To Organize Paired Reading

This chapter is in two parts. The first considers organization for parent tutoring, the second looks at the differences when organizing peer tutoring. Each of the two parts is linked with its own Planning Proforma, available on the TRW website. These are action checklists on which to record your planning decisions. They are intended to ensure that you have thought of everything and can't go wrong. You may want to look at these in the course of reading this chapter.

Organizing for parent tutoring

Not all teachers are comfortable with the idea of parental involvement in children's reading development. Some may feel that the control of the learning process should continue to reside with professionals. Others may feel that the parents of children at their school are not competent or literate or committed enough to use a technique properly. Both these views are wrong. You should however be aware that you may meet resistance as you set about organizing your project, and it is as well to have your counter arguments already marshaled.

In the first place, education must have relevance to life after school if it is to have any enduring value at all. There is little point in schools teaching children to read, if the children never read outside the school boundary. Teaching reading should include developing children's desire to read. The evidence strongly suggests that parental example has much more influence in this respect than anything teachers can do (e.g. Hewison, 1988).

In any case, many parents will try to 'help' their children at home regardless of the school's view on the matter. If the school offers no guidance to parents, many harmful practices which do indeed conflict with and sabotage the teaching in school may develop. Furthermore, the extent to which teachers actually control children's learning is doubtful. Certainly, teachers will carefully control the complexity and sequence of the educational experiences which they plan for the children, but how the children respond to these and other external experiences is up to them. Children are likely to be learning a great deal incidentally, including from other children, during the course of any experience.

Parental involvement may make teachers feel insecure. If parents start teaching children to read, it may be thought, does that imply that teachers are redundant? This is far from being the case, of course. Children will still need sophisticated teaching in language, phonic skills and grammar in school, which few parents could effectively undertake. Paired Reading does not eliminate the necessity for this kind of teaching, but does enable the teacher to delegate some of the more straightforward aspects of helping children learn to read to the parents. Paired Reading is about maximizing positive practice.

Freed from the necessity to 'hear children read' with the same degree of frequency, teachers can devote more time to refining the technical aspects of their professional work. Paired Reading complements the work teachers do in school, rather than replicating or replacing it. Also, parents need professional training and support if they are to learn to use the technique of Paired Reading properly. Teachers are clearly best placed to provide this.

If a school has only a few hours of teaching time to devote to helping children with reading, the evidence strongly suggests it will be much more cost-effective to use that time to train and support parents in the Paired Reading technique, rather than offer the children a fragmentary and irregular direct teaching service from a professional.

But surely the parents of the children who most need help will be those who are least likely to cooperate, you may say. To some extent this may be true, but experience proves it is actually very difficult to predict which parent will learn the method quickest and cooperate best. A school's view of some parents as 'inadequate' or 'uncooperative' may merely reflect the extent to which the school has already frozen the parents out of participation in their children's education.

Most professional groups can be suspicious, defensive and desirous of preserving their secret skills and mystique, and teachers are no exception. It is true that parents whose own school experiences were unhappy will have their own resistance to overcome if they are to be able to help their children, but surely schools should do all in their power to prevent continuation of the cycle of disadvantage with the next generation. Like children, parents should not be underestimated. The warmth of the reception given to parents by the school will be a crucial factor. Where a school already enjoys good relationships with the community, the establishment of a Paired Reading scheme will be much easier.

Low levels of parental literacy may not prove as large a problem as might be expected. The only real necessity is that one of the parents is a little more competent in reading than the child in question. Even if neither parent is literate, there may be a grandparent or elder brother or sister who is able to learn the technique and use it regularly. This may often apply in families where English is not the mother tongue, where the English literacy of the parents may not be good even if their capacity in oral English is adequate. Different members of different ethnic minority groups respond differentially well to Paired Reading. They are as different from each other as they are from native speakers.

Neither should it be assumed that Paired Reading is a purely 'remedial' technique. Certainly, it has proved useful with children who have made a start with reading, but do not seem to be progressing, perhaps owing to affective complications. Likewise, the child labeled 'dyslexic' may benefit. But many schools have adopted the method for use across whole year groups and age ranges, for all children of all levels of ability whose parents are interested.

So how do we set it up? A number of factors should be taken into consideration when planning the establishment of a parent-tutored Paired Reading project. These can be grouped under the headings: context, objectives, materials, recruitment, training, support and monitoring, feedback, evaluation.

Context
The first and perhaps major question is: Who has the time, energy and commitment to set it up? In any school, a minimum of two enthusiastic teachers is preferable. A single teacher who tries to set up a scheme in isolation from the rest of the staff will find it a strug-

gle, especially if the principal or head is barely tolerant of the proposal.

Secondly, consideration should be given to the nature of the school's catchment area, the degree of reading difficulty common to the pupils, the existence of minority groups whose needs may be slightly different, and the existing relationships between school and community. You also need to consider geographical ease of access to the school for parent meetings. From this will come an estimate of how much time and energy needs pouring into the project to ensure its success, or (to put it another way) how hard it is going to be.

Next, some thought about the organizational context of the school is required. What are reading standards in the school like generally? If they are alarmingly low, it may be unwise to launch a Paired Reading project, if all it serves to do is conceal fundamental flaws in the organization of reading teaching in school. Likewise, if there is division among the teaching staff, a Paired Reading project could be used as a scapegoat for one of the factions, which may be happy to see the project fail. It is worth pondering whether there are any other social or political factors which may sabotage the project.

Objectives

It is important to be clear about your objectives, since if you are not clear what outcome(s) you are hoping for you will not be able to tell whether the project has been success or not. However, life is full of surprises, so you may find some positive effects which you had not expected.

At this point, a suitable target group of children can be identified, in terms of age, reading level, class membership and numbers involved. There is a lot to be said for building in some success for a school's first experience with Paired Reading, so it would be unwise to start by targeting a large number of children with severe reading difficulties. An initial target group of a small number of children of a range of reading ability is probably the best bet.

Do not pick a few children from many different classes. It is best if the target group already has a good deal of social contact in the school. If you can involve a substantial number in the project, the children will begin to encourage and reinforce each other. Deliberately try to create a group social ethos which is positive. If children feel isolated by being labeled as Paired Readers, they may feel picked on and stigmatized. Including a wider range of reading ability in the project helps to avoid any playground prejudice that Paired Reading is for the backward. In this context you will also need to think about how the project may relate to the school's existing programs for reading teaching.

Next, some clarity must be achieved on the nature of the Paired Reading project. Is it to be a straightforward attempt to involve parents with their own children? Or would you prefer to start with something a bit less ambitious and more under the school's control, such as a scheme involving a few adult volunteers who come into school to do Paired Reading with children to whom they are not related? Such volunteers need not be parents themselves.

A scheme involving the parents of the target children is the best, however, since all kinds of positive side-effects and spin-offs accrue in this situation, in addition to improvements in reading skill.

So what sort of gains may be expected from the project? Are you hoping just for improvements in reading? Accuracy? Comprehension ? Fluency? Are you also looking for improved attitudes toward reading? Or improved attitudes to the self – greater confidence, self-esteem and so on? Or do you want to extend the children's experience of reading to different material, different places, higher levels of difficulty? Or are you using the project for other purposes, such as to improve home–school relationships generally, to give the school a better image locally, or to increase enrolment?

You do need to be honest about your objectives. Of course, you may find that different teachers who are involved actually have different objectives for the project. Subsequently one person could consider the project a success while another considers it a failure. Without honesty about objectives you can get into trouble.

Materials

If you are following the Paired Reading 'rules' to the letter, you will give children completely free choice of reading materials. However, with very young or very slow readers, or those whose parents are of limited literacy, you may want to set a readability ceiling below which the children have free choice.

In view of the increased amount of practice and increased speed of reading which is associated with the Paired Reading technique, the availability of reading material must be looked at. This raises questions about the existing quantity, quality, variety and means of access. The children's demand for reading material interesting to them may double or treble. The demand for non-fiction material is especially likely to increase.

If the school has an existing system for books to be taken home, this may need extending to all books in the school, including supplementary readers, books in classroom collections and in the school library. If you use basal readers (a 'reading scheme' in the UK), you will need to make a judgment about whether those books should be included or not (most schools decide not, and in any event the children would not choose them). The local public library may be helpful in providing a special loan collection of attractive books just for use by the Paired Reading children. Alternatively, you may be able to establish a 'special collection' for the Paired Readers from sources within school.

Information about access to local libraries should be made available to parents. You may wish to incorporate a visit to the local public library as part of your project. All kinds of reading materials should be displayed in an accessible and stimulating way. You may be able to organize other literacy-related activities during the project. The children will soon start recommending books to each other and you may wish to give them a notice board or other way of communicating their views.

The existing system for recording book loans should be scrutinized. A PR project will usually greatly increase borrowing and put a heavy strain on the current recording system, especially if it is unwieldy or elaborate. You may wish to streamline the system, give some of the work and responsibility to the children, or arrange for volunteer parents to operate the loan arrangements.

Recruitment

Assuming that a group meeting in school for parents is to be a feature of the project, communication must be established with the target parents prior to any request to attend a meeting. Preparatory information can be communicated verbally, at open or parents' evenings, and in writing in conjunction with school reports. Every opportunity to establish informal personal contact with the parents must be taken. Parents will want some idea as to why their children have been chosen, especially if the school considers their children to have reading difficulty but has never made this clear to the parents before. If you have chosen some target children at random for 'experimental' purposes, you will need to tell their parents of this.

You may wish to raise your public profile by using posters or the local media. Subsequently, letters of invitation to the initial meeting can be distributed. These should be well-designed. There should be a reply slip to give you an idea of how many to expect. A final reminder just before the meeting is likely to be necessary. There may be some value in having children write their own letters of invitation, or develop the format of the letter as a group project. Final reminders and/or persuasion via telephone will be possible with some parents.

If there are children you see as being in particular need of involvement in your project, you may wish to make special efforts to contact their parents beforehand. Perhaps a preparatory home visit would be a good investment of time if you have any at all to spare. This will be especially true in families where the parents are of limited literacy or speak English as a second or other language.

However, as has been said before, do not worry if not all the 'worst' cases in the neighborhood do not get involved in your first project. It is very important that your first is successful. Once you achieve that, the good news will ripple around the community and you will find subsequent recruitment becomes easier, with 'difficult' families more and more represented as momentum gathers.

Training

Next, ensure that the project coordinators actually know what they are talking about. They need to have not only read about Paired Reading but actually to have tried it out, preferably with a few different children. You can't talk sensibly to parents about it until you have done it yourself.

A live demonstration, or failing that a demonstration on video, is highly desirable. Contact with other local schools already using the technique, or with the local teacher resource center, school psychological service or other advisory service may provide such an opportunity. Following this, practice is necessary. The project organizers should seize any opportunity to practice the technique on a range of children, preferably not the intended target children.

It is always helpful if other staff in the school or other project centers are briefed about the method and the project. You may wish to run a brief in-service training session for your colleagues to ensure a minimal level of consistent awareness exists among them before proceeding further. Try to ensure there is an opportunity for doubts and reservations to be tabled and discussed. To help you with this, reproducible overhead masters about method and research background will be found on the TRW website.

In setting the date for your 'launch' meeting with parents and children, you need to establish the length of the initial period of the project – six, eight or ten weeks. Shorter trial periods are probably better with younger or less motivated children. Fit this neatly into a term or semester, so the active period is not broken by a long holiday.

This initial commitment creates clear expectations for tutees and tutors. It also ensures that the majority use the technique frequently enough to become both fluent and practiced in it, and also to see a significant change in the reading ability of the tutee, which should reinforce the tutors into continuing their use of the technique in the longer term.

The structure of the training for the parent and child participants must now be carefully delineated. Always have both parents and children at training meetings, so both receive exactly the same message and can practice straight away. An evening meeting may be necessary if working parents are to attend. You may have to run two parallel meetings, one during the school day and one in the evening. Most suitable times and days must be established. Avoid days with major sports events or popular TV programs. A single training meeting may suffice and minimizes parental costs of attending, or two could be considered to teach the two phases of the method separately. Consider whether you should and can provide transport and/ or child-minding facilities.

You will need to identify one major meeting room and some additional private practice spaces. It is very important that the children have already chosen books with which to practice, otherwise there will be a delay while they rush about choosing. Their class teacher should have had them choose two books prior to the meeting for practice purposes. Left to their own devices, many will choose books too easy for the appropriate practice of reading together, so check that they have at least one book which is above their independent readability level.

A warm welcome and an informal atmosphere to put everyone at their ease is essential. You may wish to offer refreshments, but do not attempt to do this in the middle of the meeting. At the beginning is OK, but at the end is best. A brief introduction can set the national and local scene, outline the objectives of the project and summarize positive evaluation results from the research literature.

Some lecturing about the PR method and its effectiveness is inevitable, but keep it brief, and avoid long words and jargon. Also avoid appearing patronizing. A video or live role play between teachers of 'How Not To Do It' may be useful to break the ice, while making some very pertinent points. Written instructions about the method, perhaps accompanied by checklists or summary guidelines for ready reference, will be necessary. Readability of these should be kept low. The standard of production should demonstrate that the project is important and professionally run. Do not give out written materials before talking, they should merely serve as a reminder of what everyone has learned.

A demonstration of how to do Paired Reading is essential, either on video, or by role play between adults, or by a live demonstration with a cooperative and socially robust child tutored by a teacher. (At subsequent meetings, parents and children who have already experienced success with the technique will be available to give demonstrations and/or offer testimonials.)

The advantages of the video are that it is easily seen and heard by a large group, which real live children may not be. Very brief clips of reading together and reading alone can be inserted at relevant points in your presentation. Choose two to three minute clips relevant to your audience. Never show a whole video program. You will bore people. Make sure the equipment is working properly for use with a large group and that you have your selected clips cued up, with any counter readings synchronized to the specific machine you are using. The video has the advantage of being predictable. Perhaps most importantly, the unknown actors can also be criticized, so you can pause and make teaching points about what has and has not happened in the sequence shown. Information about where to obtain PR training videos will be found on the TRW website.

You may wish to try making your own video. There are great advantages in having video demonstrations by local people in local accents. It helps to foster a sense of belonging and ownership. Bear in mind how the video is to be used, as detailed above. Do not try to compete with network television. You can't. Do not try to make a stand-alone self-explanatory program. It won't work and will bore people.

All you need are a few short clips of Reading Together and Reading Alone, perhaps with participants of different ages, reading levels and ethnic origin, so you can choose the most appropriate for any particular audience and intersperse them with talk. However, do not underestimate the difficulty of achieving this.

Pay careful attention to obtaining good audio. Remember people rarely do for the camera what they did in rehearsal. Fathers may be particularly difficult to recruit as movie stars. There is also the problem that if your actors do Paired Reading badly, you will not be able to critique the poor aspects for teaching purposes in front of their friends and neighbors at subsequent showings. Video role play by teachers of 'How Not To Do It' is valuable for this.

At this stage of the training meeting, it is essential to encourage all parents and children to actually practice the method before leaving. If you express this as a standard expectation, the vast majority of parents cooperate happily. If parents have not brought their children, substitute children or adult role play can be used. Teachers or other professionals can then circulate and offer praise and/or further guidance as necessary. This monitoring of practice does require a high staffing ratio – one professional is unlikely to be able to visit more than five families during a brief practice period.

Pairs who are doing well can be praised and left to continue. Pairs who are struggling may need one of three levels of further coaching. First, give further verbal advice. If that doesn't work, try joining in with the reading to model the pacing and intonation through triad reading. If all else fails, take the book and demonstrate with the child yourself, then pass the book back and let the pair continue.

Lastly, it is helpful to gather people back together and deal briefly with any other points of organization: where the children can obtain books, how often, how the monitoring system will work, what to do if there are problems, and so on. After the practice is the time for any questions from the whole group, although many parents will ask you questions individually during visits throughout practice time.

Parents and children could be asked for a verbal or written decision on whether they wish to be included in the project, and possibly also be asked to indicate preferences for alternative forms of follow-up support. Parents seldom refuse. The whole meeting should generate a lively, exciting atmosphere, so people feel they are part of a new experimental venture. Some projects hand out badges at launch meetings to foster a sense of belonging – and to turn children into walking advertisements for subsequent projects.

Support and monitoring

During the training practice session, you may wish to use the PR Technique Checklist (on the TRW website), as you circulate to see how the pairs are doing.

A most useful minimal form of monitoring is a home–school diary or recording system. Children and parents make a note of what and how much is read each night and the child takes the record sheet into school each week for the teacher to add further comments and praise. A reproducible form suitable for this purpose will be found on the TRW website.

This asks parent or child to record what has been read, for how long (so they can be praised for doing more than the minimum or restrained if they are doing too much), and with whom (so we can see how many different tutors and estimate the risk of inconsistent procedure). There is a space each day for the tutor to write a positive comment about the tutee's performance. Of course, we do not expect Paired Reading to actually happen every day.

Some tutors soon run out of good things to say. To help those with a restricted vocabulary of praise the Dictionary of Praise was devised. This will be found on the TRW website, and may be reproduced. There is also a space in the diary for the teacher or other professional to write a positive comment each week, which serves to encourage both parent and child.

The record form keeps home and school in touch and gives the child a double dose of praise from two very important sources. It also serves as a three-way accountability measure. While the teacher will see if the parents aren't doing their bit, the parents will see if the teacher hasn't bothered to sign the card or model good quality written praise. It can also serve as an emergency signaling system. If things aren't working out at home, a cry for help can be written on the card.

The easiest method for using diary cards is probably to have them color-coded by weeks, so it is easy to see if one goes astray. When the week's card has been seen by the teacher, a new color card for the ensuing week can be issued which can be stapled on to the old one. The cards thus form a cumulative record of achievement. However, do not underestimate the teacher time involved in checking the cards weekly. If you have fifteen Paired Readers in your class and you spend five minutes each per week discussing their diary cards, that amounts to an hour and a quarter per week.

Naturally, there will be some children and families for whom this relatively lightweight form of monitoring will not suffice. You may wish to schedule meetings between teachers and individual families in school to resolve any difficulties which arise, or larger group booster meetings for further practice and mutual feedback.

Visits to the homes of particularly needy families by teachers are very valuable in developing home–school relationships. They also enable professionals to see the family doing Paired Reading in their usual way in their own familiar context. The PR Technique Checklist (see TRW website) is often used by teachers in this situation. However, such visits are very expensive in teacher time and should be reserved for the most needy cases, even though all children and many parents might like them. Where home visiting is possible, a visit within the first two weeks of operation of the project is desirable. A source of funding for reimbursing travelling expenses may need locating. Some families can be asked to rate their own performance against the PR Technique Checklist.

Some form of follow-up support and monitoring for the coordinating teacher(s) is also desirable, especially where the project is a first attempt or the project leader is professionally isolated. Support may come from mentors within school, or perhaps better still from an external consultant. Teachers should proactively recruit support of this kind.

Feedback

Parental involvement in children's reading is a collaborative venture between the three main participants – teachers, parents and children. If the initiative is to become self-sustaining and grow, all three parties need to feel valued and appreciated, consulted and empowered.

It is therefore important that after the stipulated initial trial or experimental period of Paired Reading, parents and children share their views on the degree of success of the venture. At this point they also need to make their own decision about where they are going to go from here. Some families may choose to go on doing Paired Reading several days a week, others less frequently. Some may wish to try another kind of approach to reading at home, some may wish to try parental involvement in another curriculum area such as spelling (see Part Four of this book), while a few may wish to stop altogether.

Feedback meetings may include parents and children all together or separately. More mature children may cope well with the former (remember PR makes them more confident), but younger children should perhaps have a separate meeting at which their views are gathered by a professional. Parents and children can then meet up to hear the professional's summary of both sets of views. You may expect to hear many contradictory opinions expressed at such meetings. Remember that it is important that they have a chance to give their views – that in itself has valuable effects. You may end up feeling that you cannot possibly follow all the contradictory advice given about making improvements, however.

The feedback meeting can be much more relaxed and informal than the training meeting. The professionals should give their feedback to the parents first, modeling the appropriate behavior. Urge those who are usually quiet in meetings to offer a comment, however brief. If you have evaluation results for your project at this time, report them in summary to the parents. Do not give data about individual children. Specific test scores are probably best avoided except in private discussion with the pair themselves, and maybe not even then if the individual's scores are potentially misleading.

You will want to celebrate the success of the children, parents and school. Schools have their own styles on these matters. Some form of certificate is often well received, or perhaps an even grander badge.

Very often parents will appreciate these as well. A reproducible certificate for this purpose will be found on the TRW website.

If you wish to discuss possible modifications to the Paired Reading procedure for those pairs who feel ready to move on, the reproducible handout Beyond Paired Reading (see TRW website) may be useful.

Evaluation

There is considerable virtue in building in some form of evaluation for the initial experimental period of the project. This is especially true when the project is a first for the school. The evaluation of Paired Reading projects is considered in detail in Chapter 5.

Naturally, the first project a school runs is the most difficult and consumes the most energy. Once the teachers involved are familiar with the procedure, and all the required materials are at hand, the project can be run for subsequent target groups with much less work.

Organizing for peer tutoring

Many of the planning considerations relevant for parent tutoring are also relevant for peer tutoring. If you have turned directly to this section you should go to the beginning of the chapter and read the whole. What follows largely covers the different or additional planning aspects for peer tutoring. These are divided into subsections: context and objectives, materials, selection and matching, organization of contact, training, support and monitoring, feedback, and evaluation.

Context and objectives

Contextual strengths and weakness will need assessing for a peer tutor project in a way very similar to that for a parent tutor project. Although it is possible to operate a peer tutor reading project entirely within the confines of your own classroom, some support from colleagues inside or outside school is highly desirable to maximize the chance of a successful first project. At the very least, the agreement of the principal is essential. If this is a new venture for the school, advice and support from more experienced teacher colleagues in other local schools or specialist advisory agencies should be sought.

Careful consideration should be given to potential problems which are specific to your individual school. There may be difficulties with a large proportion of ethnic minority pupils, or with massive reading problems in a particular age group, or a problem of the pupils being so alienated from the aims of institutional education that initially they feel unable to play the part of tutor comfortably. If you feel that reading standards in the school are, in general, lower than they should be, take especial care. It is very important that peer tutor projects are not used to compensate for, and thereby perhaps disguise, fundamental weaknesses in the professional teaching of reading within a school.

It is also important that teachers do not see in peer tutoring a means of giving children extra reading practice while they remain under the direct supervision and control of a professional as an alternative to the possibly more challenging development of involving the parents in this exercise at home. Parents acting as reading helpers at home have great strengths, as well as weaknesses, in this role which are different to those of either peer tutors or professional teachers.

Teachers will run peer tutor projects for very different purposes, and a success for one teacher could be construed as a failure by another with different objectives. Objectives need to be realistic.

It is reasonable to expect both tutors and tutees to show increased accuracy and fluency of reading, better comprehension, and increased confidence and love of literature. It is not reasonable to expect a brief project to completely resolve a long-standing reading problem in the school.

Peer tutor projects often include social gains among their objectives. Thus in a cross-age project, one aim may be to increase a sense of cohesiveness and caring between older and younger children. In a project which matches children across genders, races, or other differences, familiarization may also yield social benefits.

Peer tutoring should also be characterized by explication of objectives for the tutors. Well organized peer tutoring should involve learning by teaching for the tutors, who should also gain in terms of reading skills, attitudes, and self-esteem. If you cannot specify valid educational objectives for the tutors you are merely using them, and their parents will rightly object to this.

Reading materials

Remember that controlling the readability of the material used to the tutee's current independent readability level fails to challenge the tutee and runs the risk of boring the tutor. However, the readability of the material should certainly have a ceiling placed upon it at the tutor's independent reading level. We must avoid at all costs the tutee presenting the tutor with failure, or the generation of confusion through both tutee and tutor losing touch with the text.

Where there is a large reading ability difference between tutor and tutee, the readability of the material may need controlling to a point somewhat below the tutor's level, but still above the tutee's level. However, avoid big ability differentials wherever possible. The tutor will certainly gain more and remain more interested if the reading ability differential is only two or three years. This is discussed further on p. 40.

While some books in school may already be graded for readability, and pairs can thereby easily ensure that tutors are not over-challenged, once the pair begins to explore more widely the issue of readability can become more problematic. Pairs should be taught a simple way of checking readability. It should be made perfectly clear to them why they need to know and implement this. As children become more used to choosing and to each other, they will develop their own more sophisticated methods, about which you can hold a class discussion.

When given free choice, many children develop or learn the skills of choosing appropriately within two or three weeks, and teachers should avoid interfering during the early period of a project in this respect. However a small minority of children may still be all at sea about choosing appropriate books even after this time, and at this juncture teachers may need to step in to give a little gentle assistance and guidance, the aim being to develop choosing skills in the child rather than merely doing it for the child.

As with parent tutoring, the sources for reading materials can be many and various. The number of books that the children get through will amaze you, and ideally they should be able to change their books on every occasion they are in contact. It may be logistically easier to mount a special additional collection in some convenient area.

Some children will wish to bring in books or magazines from home, and this should certainly be encouraged up to a point provided the readability level remains within the tutor's competence. Some children may begin bringing in comics, which may be accepted up to a point, but if it gets out of hand be prepared to impose a quota.

Selection and matching of children

All teachers have experienced the great variations in general maturity level shown by classes in succeeding years. It would be particularly unwise to mount a project involving many children where the maturity of many children to cope with the procedure is in grave doubt. In cases of uncertainty it is usually wisest to start a small pilot project with a few of the most mature children in the class acting as tutors, to enable further tutors to be added to the project as a privilege.

Where the children have already been used to taking a degree of responsibility for their own learning and/or working on cooperative projects in small groups, they may be expected to take to peer tutoring more readily. The gender balance in the class can represent a problem, particularly if there are more girls than boys, since some boys may express extreme reluctance at the prospect of being tutored by a girl. Needless to say, this reluctance often disappears fairly quickly in class where the teacher allocates a female tutor to a male tutee and instructs them to get on with it, but the unfortunate tutee may still have difficulty justifying what is going on to his friends in the playground.

The chronological age of the tutors and tutees needs considering separately. Do not assume that age and ability are synonymous. If you intend to use tutors who are considerably older than the tutees, unless you are fortunate enough to teach a vertically grouped class, you are likely to find the organization of the project considerably more complicated. This is especially true if the tutors are to be imported from another school. Same-age tutoring within one class is by far the easiest to organize.

Consideration of the overall number of pupils to be involved is also necessary. Start with a small number of children in the target group. Resist any temptation to include just one more, or before you know where you are the whole thing will become unmanage-able. Particularly for a first venture, it is important to be able to clo-sely monitor a small number of children. Do not worry about those who have to be excluded. They can have a turn later, or be incorpo-rated into the project as your organization becomes more fluent and automatic. Also, if any evaluation is to be carried out, it will be useful to also check the progress of a comparison group of children who have not been involved in the peer tutoring.

The reading ability of the children is the critical factor in selection and matching of tutors and tutees. As we have said, as a general rule it is probably as well to keep a differential of about two years reading age between tutors and tutees. Where same-age tutoring is to be established with a whole class, the children can be ranked in terms of scores on reading tests, and a line drawn through the middle of the ranked list to separate tutors at the top from tutees at the bottom. Then the most able tutor is paired with the most able tutee, and so on. Other criteria for ranking could include basal reader (reading scheme) level or the teacher's observations or intuitive judgment.

However, the children's reading ability is not the only factor which must be taken into account. Pre-existing social relationships in the peer group must also be considered. To pair children with their best friend of the moment may not be a good idea, particularly as the friendship may be of short duration. Obviously it would be undesir-able to pair a child with another child with whom there is a pre-exist-ing poor relationship. Another of the advantages of a same-age project is that one teacher is much more likely to know all the chil-dren involved, and thus can be more sensitive in taking social rela-tionships into account.

It may or may not be desirable to take the individual preferences of the children themselves into account in some way. Some children may surprise you with the maturity they show in selecting a tutor they think would be effective. However, to allow completely free child selection of tutor is likely to result in chaos. Some tutors would be over-chosen, others not chosen at all, quite apart from the ques-tion of maintaining the requisite differential in reading ability.

One of the organizational difficulties with peer tutoring is the impact of absence from school of a tutor or tutee. It is always worth-while to nominate a spare, standby or supply tutor or two, to ensure that a tutor's absence can be covered. Children acting as spare tutors need to be particularly stable, sociable and competent at reading, since they will have to work with a wide range of tutees. However, do not worry about imposing a burden on the spare tutors, as they may be expected to benefit the most in terms of increases in reading ability and self-esteem. The other obvious strategy for coping with absence is to attempt to rematch the children without partners, perhaps involving a change of role for some.

The question of parental agreement often arises in connection with peer tutor projects. Experience shows that involvement in such a project is usually sufficiently interesting for the children to result in many of them mentioning it at home. This can result in some parents getting very strange ideas about what is going on. It is thus usually desirable for a brief note from school to be taken home by both tutors and tutees, explaining the project very simply. The TRW website includes a specimen leaflet for parents about peer assisted learning. This should reassure parents that the project will have both academic and social benefits for tutors as well as tutees.

Organization of contact

A basic decision is whether the tutoring is to occur wholly in class time, wholly in the children's break or recess time, or in a combination of both.

If the tutoring is to occur wholly in class time, it can be kept under teacher supervision. However, it will usually require scheduling. If the tutoring is to occur in the children's break time, more mature pairs can be left to make their own arrangements. This arrangement is a much greater imposition on tutors and tutees alike, however, and the momentum of the project may begin to slow as the novelty begins to wear off. Some scheduling may thus be necessary even during the children's recess time, so that the size and nature of the commitment involved is visible to all from the outset. The best compromise is usually to schedule some minimum of contact for class time (perhaps three sessions per week), but allow the opportunity for pairs to do additional tutoring in their own break time if they so wish.

Finding the physical space to accommodate the pairs can be a problem. In a cross-age project, particularly where two full classes are involved, it is possible for half the pairs to work in the tutees' class-room and the other half in the tutors' classroom. Finding physical space for the tutoring to occur during recess times may be consider-ably more difficult if there are problems of supervision or children are not allowed access to classrooms.

Each individual tutoring period should last for a minimum of fifteen minutes. Little worthwhile can occur in less time than this, after you have allowed for lack of punctuality and general settling down. If it is possible for the really enthusiastic to continue for over twenty minutes, this is advantageous. It may be possible for the minimum fifteen minutes to occur just before a natural break time, but provide for the possibility of children continuing into their own break time if they so desire.

The frequency of tutorial contact should be three times each week as a basic minimum to ensure that the project has a significant and measurable impact. If peer tutoring occurs less frequently, it may have benefits, but they may not be measurable. If four or five con-tacts per week can be arranged, so much the better. Children involved in peer tutor projects rarely object to daily tutoring, as most of them find it interesting and rewarding. Some pairs may organize their own impromptu sessions in their own break times.

The project should be launched with reference to an initial fixed period of commitment. It is useful for both tutors and tutees to be clear about what they are letting themselves in for, and how long a course they need to be able to sustain. A minimum project period of six weeks is suggested, since it will barely be possible to discern sig-nificant impact in less time than this. Popular project periods are eight weeks and ten weeks, which fit comfortably within an average term or semester.

It is not desirable to fix a period of longer than twelve weeks for an initial commitment. It will be much better to review the project at the end of a short initial period, to evaluate the outcomes and make decisions about future directions jointly with the children, rather than letting the whole thing drift on interminably until it runs out of steam.

Training
It is neither effective nor ethically justifiable to turn the tutors loose

on the unsuspecting tutees without giving them some form of training. Just as with parent tutoring, before teachers set out to train children in particular procedures it is important that the teachers
themselves are well practiced in the method to be used. Sometimes
the tutors and tutees are trained in two separate groups, but it is best
to train them together. As with parent training, the format of introduction, talk, demonstration, practice, feedback and coaching, questions, organizational details and written information should be
followed. See pp. 29–33 for details.

Support and monitoring

During the course of the project, it is important that the coordinating teacher keeps a close eye on how things are going, in order to nip
any incipient problems in the bud. In the spirit of cooperation which
permeates peer tutoring, the children themselves may be the first to
report difficulty or seek help. Such self-referral may revolve around
asking the meaning of words which are unfamiliar to both tutor and
tutee. Children also should be encouraged to readily report difficulties in accommodating to each other's habits without feeling that
they are telling tales.

Where a supervising teacher is present during the tutoring, much
can be gleaned by observing individual pairs in rotation. The peer
tutoring session is not an opportunity for the teacher to get on with
some marking. On the contrary, the teacher should either be setting
a good example by reading silently or with a tutee, or (preferably)
should be circulating round the group observing and guiding children as necessary. It is possible to ask a particularly expert child tutor
(perhaps a standby tutor) who is not otherwise engaged, to act as an
observer in a similar way and report back to the teacher. The PR
Technique Checklist (on the TRW website) will be useful for both
teachers and peer monitors to help structure the observations. This
checklist can also be used as a self-assessment device by more mature
pairs.

Some form of self-recording of each session during the project is
probably desirable. It is a tangible demonstration of achievement for
the children and of considerable interest for the monitoring teacher.
It is entirely logical that these records should be kept by the children
themselves. Simple diaries like those for parent projects can be kept

by each pair (see PR Diary on the TRW website). The tutee can record date and book read, while the tutor records some words of praise or other comment. The pair can refer to the Dictionary of Praise (on the TRW website) as necessary.

Even quite young children acting as tutors can prove to be surprisingly good at writing positive comments about their tutees. Learning to give and receive praise without embarrassment is a valuable component of peer tutor projects. The diaries are checked each week by the supervising teacher, who can also record some favorable comment and add an official signature if required.

In addition, it is often worthwhile calling occasional review meetings with tutors and tutees separately or together, in order to discuss how the project is going and what improvements could be made.

Feedback

A simple way of presenting the favorable results and information to the children themselves is necessary to encourage them and promote further growth of confidence. A more scientific account will be necessary for interested colleagues. The information for this need not necessarily be more complex, merely different in emphasis.

At the end of the initial phase of the project, in the light of the evaluation and monitoring information, joint decisions have to be made about the future. At this point, the views of the children must be taken into account. Some may want to continue peer tutoring with the same frequency, others may wish to continue but with a lesser frequency, while a few may be wanting a complete rest, at least for a while.

When in doubt, a good rule of thumb is to go for the parsimonious option. It will be better to leave some of the children a little hungry, and have them pestering you to launch another project in six weeks time, rather than let peer tutoring meander on indefinitely until it quietly expires. At this point of decision-making also beware of trying to cater for a wide variety of choices from different tutoring pairs. The organization of the project could become unbelievably complicated if you attempt to accommodate the varying desires for continuation of large numbers of children. It is probably as well to stick with what the majority vote for. Peer tutoring can thus be seen to be not only cooperative, but democratic as well.

Evaluation

As with parent tutoring, there is considerable virtue in building in some form of evaluation for the initial trial period. This is especially true where the project is a first for the school.

The evaluation of Paired Reading projects is considered in detail in Chapter 5.

4 Does Paired Reading Work?

Paired Reading is one of the most intensively evaluated interventions in education. There has been a great deal of research on PR, particularly in the UK, US, Canada, Australia and New Zealand. By the early 1990s, PR had been the subject of hundreds of studies. These were reviewed by Topping and Lindsay (1992b) and Topping (1995a). The 1995 review is available in full on the TRW website, complete with all references. The TRW website also contains overhead masters summarizing the evaluation research on PR, useful for any presentations you may wish to make. This chapter will summarize the research on PR up until 1995 briefly, and discuss the research after 1995 in more detail.

Paired Reading is also one of the most effective interventions in education. In a recent review of the effectiveness of twenty interventions in reading, Paired Reading ranked as one of the most effective, surpassed only by one or two methods which seemed to have produced spectacular results, but which had only been evaluated with very small numbers of children in research projects (Brooks *et al.*, 1998). By contrast, Paired Reading has been demonstrated to be effective with thousands of children in hundreds of schools in many countries. Additionally, implementing Paired Reading typically involves very modest additional costs in time and materials, with strong implications for relative cost-effectiveness.

Outcome research

Much of the evaluation research has been in terms of gains on norm-referenced tests of reading before and after the initial intensive period of involvement. The general picture in published studies is that Paired Readers progress at about 4.2 times normal rates in reading accuracy on test during the initial period of commitment. Thus, for example, Paired Reading for a three-month period was associated on average with gains in reading accuracy normally expected over a period of $3 \times 4.2 = 12.6$ months (although this is only an approximation, since it cannot be assumed that reading development is linear, and one month of gain in reading age would not mean the same from different reading age baselines). Gains in reading comprehension were even greater.

The research literature suggests that follow-up gains may vary considerably from school to school. Continued acceleration at above normal rates is relatively rare, and indeed some follow-up gains cited are less than normal rates, while still remaining better than those of control or comparison groups. Follow-up periods have been very various, ranging from four weeks to twelve months, but the length of follow-up does not appear to relate consistently to the favorability of follow-up findings. However, there is little suggestion here of wash-out of experimental gains. There is evidence that acceleration can be sustained and even increased with the deployment of different types of tutor consecutively, and that changes in reading style can also endure in the long term.

Nor are these results confined to isolated and possibly atypical research projects, or to studies published in journals that may have a bias toward studies finding positive and statistically significant results. In the Kirklees school district in Yorkshire in the UK, the technique has been used by a majority of schools. This enabled study of outcomes in all projects in all schools. These unselected results are likely to give a much more realistic picture of likely outcomes in an average school under normal conditions.

In a sample of 2372 children in 155 projects run by many different schools, average test gains of 3.3 times normal rates in reading accuracy and 4.4 times normal rates in reading comprehension were found. Although somewhat lower than the average from the research literature, this still represents a very substantial effect. It was this effect size that the Brooks *et al.* (1998) review compared with effect sizes from other interventions, not the higher effect sizes for PR indicated by the published literature (1.41 to 2.12).

The Kirklees results were supported by substantial baseline and control group data. In 23 baselined projects incorporating 374 Paired Readers who acted as their own controls, the difference between

baseline (no-PR) and PR period gains was highly statistically significant. In 37 control or comparison group projects studies incorporating 580 Paired Readers and 446 control children, the difference
between PR and control group gains was highly statistically significant in both reading accuracy and comprehension.

At short-term and long-term follow-up the gains of Paired Readers
remained at above normal rates on average, with no sign of wash out.
At short-term follow-up (less than seventeen weeks), 102 children in
seven projects were still progressing at 2.0 times normal rates of gain
in reading accuracy, 2.3 times in reading comprehension. At long-term
follow-up (seventeen weeks to over one year), 170 children in ten projects were still progressing at 1.2 times normal rates of gain in reading
accuracy, 1.4 times in reading comprehension (see Topping, 1992a).

Children from all social classes were involved in projects, 60 per
cent of participants being of below-average socio-economic status
for the school district, which was itself disadvantaged. There was a
tendency for participants of lower socio-economic status to make
larger gains in reading accuracy, even if not home visited. However,
home-visiting made an additional significant positive difference for
participants in the lowest quartile of socio-economic status. There
are implications here for the cost-effectiveness of differential inclusion of home-visiting support in this kind of service delivery (see
Topping and Lindsay, 1992c).

Children from families speaking English as a second or other language were recorded in 50 projects yielding norm-referenced data,
operated in 30 schools. Compared to Paired Readers for whom English was a first language, the ESOL children made greater gains in
accuracy (but not statistically significantly) and significantly smaller
gains in comprehension, although the cultural relevance of the reading tests must be questioned (see Topping, 1992b).

More data were available for parent-tutored than peer-tutored
projects, but no significant difference in outcomes between the
two was found. The evidence suggested that peer tutors tended to
gain more than tutees, although this difference did not reach statistical significance. There was less follow-up research on peer tutoring
than parent tutoring. PR had also been used successfully with children with severe learning difficulties and other special needs and in
further education and adult literacy.

Taking another approach to evaluation, the subjective views of tutors, tutees and teachers in the unselected projects were also gathered by structured questionnaire (Topping and Whiteley, 1990). In a sample of over 1000 tutors, after PR 70 per cent considered their tutee was now reading more accurately, more fluently and with better comprehension. Greater confidence in reading was noted by 78 per cent of tutors. Teachers reported generalized reading improvement in a slightly smaller proportion of cases. Of a sample of 964 tutees, 95 per cent felt that after PR they were better at reading and 92 per cent liked reading more. Eighty-seven per cent found it easy to learn to do, 83 per cent liked doing it and 70 per cent said they would go on doing it.

Reading style studies

Considering parent- and peer-tutored studies together, in eight studies error rates have been found to reduce with PR and in no study have error rates increased. In seven studies Paired Readers showed decreases in refusal rates and in two studies an increase. In seven studies use of context showed an increase, in one case no difference was found, and in no case was there a decrease. In four studies the rate or speed of reading showed an increase and in no case was there a decrease. In four studies, self-correction rate showed an increase and in no case a decrease. In three studies the use of phonics showed an increase and in no case was there a decrease. Although many of the differences cited did not reach statistical significance and only a few studies used either control or comparison groups that were non-participant or used another technique, strong consistent trends emerge from all these studies considered together.

The general pattern is of Paired Reading resulting in fewer refusals (greater confidence), greater fluency, greater use of context and a greater likelihood of self-correction, as well as fewer errors and better phonic skills.

Studies of compliance to technique

In studies of compliance to PR technique, many contradictory findings are evident for both parent-tutored and peer-tutored projects. High levels of compliance appear to be more likely in studies of smaller numbers of participants, especially when the training has been more detailed. In larger studies of parent-tutored PR at home, conformity to good technique has been found in from 75 per cent to 43 per cent of participants, the higher figure being associated with home visits. Elliott and Hewison (1994) found that, even a year after training, PR working-class parents showed greater comprehension-related discussion, more frequent rapid correction after brief pause, and less phonic correction compared to an untrained working-class group. The working-class PR children could read as well as the middle-class children, while the untrained working-class children lagged behind.

The amount of time spent doing Paired Reading generally does seem to not correlate highly with measured outcomes, although measuring time on task in home-based projects is particularly difficult. Extra practice is clearly only one of the pathways through which PR has its effects. The majority of studies have evaluated on a crude input-output model, and the relation between technique compliance and outcome remains somewhat obscure.

Studies directly comparing alternative methods

Of 22 studies directly experimentally comparing Paired Reading to other techniques, in eighteen cases statistical significance of findings is given, and in seven of these Paired Reading significantly out-performed other techniques. A number of other studies found Paired Reading superior but the difference did not attain statistical significance in small samples. No study found Paired Reading significantly inferior. In the fifteen studies yielding adequate norm-referenced data, the mean pre–post multiple of normal rates of gain in reading accuracy for Paired Readers was 3.9 and that for other techniques 2.7.

A meta-analytic approach to comparing methods

Alternatively, a meta-analytic approach to comparison could be pursued, comparing effect sizes in all Paired Reading studies with effect sizes in all studies using each specific alternative technique. Unfortunately, attempts to meta-analyse the literature on studies of 'hearing' or 'listening to children read' approaches quickly run into difficulties. Of the major studies in the UK, one (Hewison and Tizard, 1980) found statistically significant effects, sustained at follow-up, while the other (Hannon, 1987) failed to find statistically significant effects.

A large proportion of the other literature on hearing/listening approaches fails to offer a precise description of what tutors were asked to do or actually did, and numerical outcome data are often conspicuous by their absence. However, crudely aggregating fourteen published hearing/listening studies where reading test data are given (total n = 290) yields an average pre-post multiple of normal progress of 2.53, compared to the PR literature average of 4.23. This latter finding on relative effectiveness is supported by reviews by Toomey (1991, 1993).

More recent studies

Law and Kratochwill (1993) reported on a parent-tutored program during the summer school vacation that incorporated very unusual recruitment, training and assessment procedures. No statistically significant improvement in reading accuracy or fluency from baseline to post-intervention was evident (although sample size was very small). However, the parents reported that the PR technique had a positive effect on their children's reading skills, particularly increased confidence, interest, enjoyment and expressiveness. The majority of the children also rated the method highly.

Miller and Kratochwill (1996) recruited by repeatedly soliciting parents of the students qualifying for Chapter 1 services (a federal funding project) in two schools. Parents were trained individually, but several parents insisted on postponing training, while many others reported difficulty getting started and continuing consistently. Many of the participating parents and students failed to cooperate fully. The subset of children in the PR condition who actually completed the program did show significantly greater gains in accuracy and comprehension than their matched controls. These two studies illustrate the need to pay careful attention to organizational issues of implementation.

A number of more regular positive reports of PR in both peer- and parent-tutored formats have originated from the US (e.g. De-Angelo, 1997; Leach, 1993). An updated search of the ERIC database will reveal many reports in peer reviewed journals and elsewhere, with the advantage that items not published in easily available journals or books can be obtained worldwide from the ERIC Document Reproduction Service. However, readers will find that a number of studies combined PR with other interventions, so the impact of PR alone is not clarified.

Winter (1996) compared a peer-tutored PR class and a comparison silent independent reading (equivalent time on task at reading) class in each of three English-medium primary schools in Hong Kong. These children were very able readers. The PR tutees chose easy reading material, which they could read quickly with few errors. Unsurprisingly error correction was very low. Nevertheless, the PR groups made much bigger reading test gains than the comparison silent reading class. Topping (1997b) has responded to issues raised by Winter.

The first published study on PR from South America (Cupolillo *et al.*, 1997) sought to evaluate the PR procedure with children who were repeating first grade, in an area of northern Brazil where 55 per cent of the population were illiterate. Tutors included parents, relatives and peers, but all tutoring took place in homes. The project was evaluated in terms of tutee changes in reading fluency, comprehension, confidence and reading habits. Gains were evident for those who had participated consistently, especially in confidence and reading habits. This novel use of PR with young emergently literate children in a different cultural context (and continent) was ground-breaking. Some adaptation of the method was involved.

A PR program in a disadvantaged community in Cape Town, South Africa, was reported by Overett and Donald (1998). Parents and other family members served as tutors for students in English-medium classes. Experimental and control children were on average a year behind their chronological age in reading accuracy, and two years in reading comprehension. More than half the children reported there were no books in the home, and of the remainder very few had more than two. Experimental and control classes received equivalent loans of books, and class teachers encouraged both groups to join the library. Compared to the control group, the PR group made statistically significant improvements in reading accuracy and comprehension, as well as reading attitude. Relationships between tutees and tutors improved, and other children in the families seemed to benefit also. Interactions between family, school and the local library were enhanced. Smith and Johnson (1995) reviewed the impact of Paired Reading in South African primary schools.

Murad and Topping (2000) reported a further study in Brazil, with children in first grade for the first time, but in a relatively advantaged private school setting. All tutors were parents, and a control group took equivalent books home to read with their parents, but had no PR training. Although similar at pre-test, PR children were significantly superior to their controls at post-test, especially in relation to the deeper complexities of the logical sequence and meaning of the text. Autonomous reading fluency was also higher for the PR group. There were indications that the affective and self-efficacy components of PR were particularly important.

The Read On project in Scotland

In the Paired Reading phase of the pilot Paired Reading and Thinking project in Scotland, the equivalent of 32 full classes in thirteen schools were involved in cross-age peer tutoring. Older elementary school students (around ten or eleven years old) tutored younger students (seven or eight years old). Pairs met three times per week for twenty minutes per session over a ten-week period.

For tutees in sixteen full classes, nine classes showed average gains well above normal which reached statistical significance, six classes showed gains above normal which did not reach statistical significance, and one class showed only normal gains. For tutors in sixteen full classes, seven classes showed gains well above normal which reached statistical significance, eight classes showed gains above normal which did not reach statistical significance, and one class showed only normal gains. The majority of children in this project were in schools in disadvantaged areas, and their average score before the project started was well below average in many cases – in other words, what was a normal rate of gain for most children was not normal for them. The aggregated gains for all tutors were highly statistically significant. The same was true for the tutees.

A minority of schools were able to provide non-participant

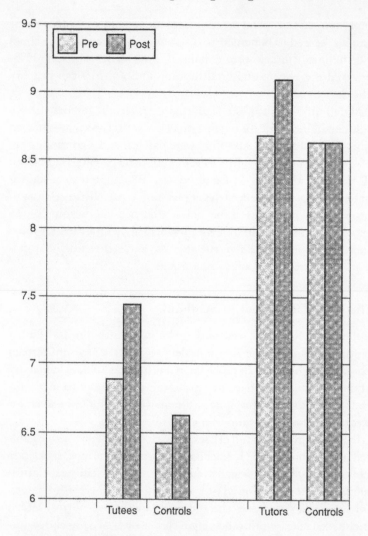

Figure 1   Pre-post reading age gains for tutees and tutors, and their
controls

control or comparison groups of the same age for either tutors or
tutees. One school managed to provide both (see Figure 1). Both
PR tutors and tutees out-performed their respective controls.

An analysis was conducted of the relationship between pre-test
reading ability and amount of reading test gain. Overall, the least

able tutees and the least able tutors gained most. Low ability tutors produced tutee gains at least equivalent to those produced by high ability tutors, and low ability tutors themselves gained more than high ability tutors.

The relationship between reading gains and sex was also analysed. Overall, girl tutees did better than boys, but boy tutors did better than girls in terms of their own test gains. Perhaps boys learn better by being tutors than by being tutored. Teachers had been encouraged to match children by ability differential, disregarding sex, but nevertheless cross-sex matching proved to be less usual. However, cross-sex matching actually yielded better tutee gains than same-sex matching, and was good for tutors as well. Boy–boy pairs appeared very good for the tutor, but not for the tutee (contrary to previous findings of high gains for both partners in this constellation; see Topping and Whiteley, 1993). Girl–girl pairs did least well on aggregate.

Social gains were also widely reported. Participating teachers were asked to record their summary observations of child behavior. They were asked to comment only on children in their class whose reading they knew before Paired Reading started, and only indicate change if they had observed it, it was significant, and it had definitely occurred since PR started. The response rate was 33 out of 34 (one teacher had left the school). The summary results are displayed in Figure 2 for behavior in the classroom during Paired Reading, and in Figure 3 for behavior in other activities in the classroom and outside the classroom within school.

It is clear that for behavior in the classroom during Paired Reading, very few teachers had not observed a positive shift in the majority of their children. Regarding generalization of positive effects to other subject areas and outside the classroom, the effects were not as strong (as would be expected), but were still positive. The improvement in motivation during the PR sessions was particularly striking. Especially worthy of note was the improvement in ability to relate to each other. Their social competence improved both during PR and beyond it.

The Read On website (www.dundee.ac.uk/psychology/ReadOn) at the Centre for Paired Learning at the University of Dundee has further information about this project.

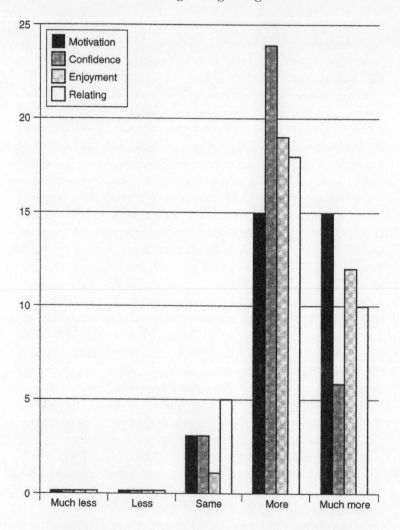

Figure 2 Teacher observations: during the PR sessions

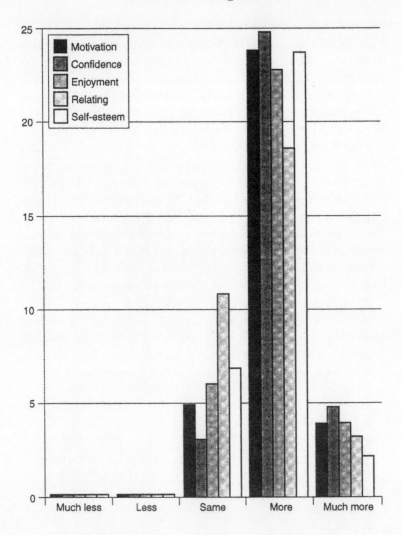

Figure 3 Teacher observations: outside the PR sessions

Summary and conclusion

Paired Reading works – in terms of raising scores on many kinds of reading tests and improving attitudes to reading. There is evidence that these gains are sustained. Paired Reading has demonstrated a high degree of durability, replicability and generalizability in a wide

variety of contexts in several different countries. Despite methodo-
logical weakness in some of the reported studies, the better quality
studies have shown no less encouraging results than the rest. In any
event the sheer volume of multiple-site replication is impressive.

Paired Reading generally works better than regular class teaching
alone, and better than supplementary silent reading or peer- or
home-based listening to reading approaches.

Exactly why and how Paired Reading works remains somewhat
mysterious. Positive changes in reading style have been noted in
Paired Readers, but it is not clear whether these are causes, effects,
or mediating mechanisms. However, the conception of PR as a uni-
tary intervention may be over-simplistic. The PR experience may
offer participants multiple pathways to improvements in multiple
aspects of the reading process. Different components of the technique may be most potent for different readers, reducing the probability of finding a few process factors which are omnipotent for all.

Recommendations for further research include more multiple-site
field trials. This is increasingly occurring in an international context.
Meanwhile, it may be concluded that Paired Reading has certainly
been better evaluated than many educational innovations.

It has been argued that community interventions should be:

- simple
- inexpensive
- effective
- compatible with the existing values and need structures of
  the population
- flexible
- decentralized
- sustainable.

The research on Paired Reading is generally most encouraging, and
suggests that in a context of well-organized delivery the technique is
capable of meeting all of these requirements.

5 How To Evaluate Paired Reading

Just because spectacular results have been achieved in some places, that does not guarantee you will get them right there where you are. Especially with your first effort, you need to know how successful you have been – and how you can improve.

Then circumstances will change or you will want to do something a little differently, so evaluation remains important. Evaluation will also help convince skeptics of the value of what you are doing. Carrying out your own evaluation is a lot more comfortable than some outsider imposing it upon you. You will also find the tutors and tutees very eager to be told how well they have done, so you had better have something concrete to tell them!

One of the great virtues of Paired Reading is its cost-effectiveness, so it would be nonsensical to spend a vast amount of time on evaluation. However, it is worth devoting some time to this task. You will need to choose the ways you think are best and easiest for your own situation. First, you need to think clearly about evaluation design.

Evaluation design

The obvious thing is to apply some measure like a reading test at the beginning and end of the project (pre- and post-test). But if your measure is not norm-referenced (standardized), you will have no way of telling whether the children would have made the changes anyway, irrespective of the project. Even if your measure is norm-referenced, unless your results are spectacularly better than normal rates of gain, you still will not have evidence that the children could only have made those gains with PR.

So you really need to compare the progress of your project children with the progress of a similar group who have not been involved in the project – a control or comparison group. A true control group is identical to the experimental group in every way (including pre-test attainment, age, sex balance). Random allocation to experimental and control groups is often suggested to be the most scientific way of equalizing the two groups. However, with small numbers, random allocation sometimes yields groups that are not actually identical. Also, few tutoring organizers find it very practical.

Think carefully about relevant ways in which your two groups are different. Different teachers? Different amounts of time on task at reading? Have the experimental group selected themselves by volunteering? If you are comparing them with a group that has self-selected not to participate, motivational differences between the groups seem likely.

One of the problems with control groups is that their use seems to involve denying a service or facility to people who are in need of it, at least in the short run. You can justify this on the grounds that you do not have the resources to help everyone at the same time effectively, and random allocation is fairer than other methods of rationing. It can also be argued that until you have demonstrated that the project has actually worked by using the control group, you don't know whether you are denying the control group anything worthwhile.

Alternatively, think about a time series or baseline design. For instance, if a school has a regular routine of giving reading tests, historical data may be available for the project group. This enables you to scrutinize the fluctuations in progress in the past, and see how the gains during the project compare. In a sense, each person serves as her or his own control over time. Where the regular trend of time series data is interrupted by a special event like a Paired Reading project, you check to see what sort of a blip in the trend emerges. You could even combine a control/comparison group with a baseline/time series, giving a baseline or time series with comparison series. It is advantageous if the time series can be continued after the end of the project. This will generate very interesting and valuable long-term follow-up data.

One further design is probably worth mentioning here, the multiple baseline. If a larger group of potential pupils exists than can participate at one time, you may provide two consecutive projects. In this case it is reasonable and fair to allocate children to the first and second groups randomly.

Teachers will often do this when a whole class of 30 wants to do Paired Reading but it is clear that there is not enough time to look at 30 diary cards each week. It is better to work with half of the class properly at one time, rather than overload and stress the system. The second group will be all the more enthusiastic for having their appetite whetted. Quite often the second group makes bigger gains than the first group.

So in the short term you compare the gains of the first group to those of the non-participant second group. In the medium term you compare the gains of the now participant second group to their own progress before participating, and to the progress of the early group when participating. You can also collect post-participation follow-up data on the first group and compare it to their own gains while participating. In the longer term you can collect post-participation follow-up data on the second group and compare it to the follow-up data on the first group as well as to their own participation gains. You can also collect longer term follow-up data on the first group and compare that to their shorter term follow-up data. Try drawing this on a graph of time against reading test scores.

Whatever you choose to do, think about the possibility of the Hawthorne effect. This is when participants in a study show brief improvement purely because some attention is being paid to them and there is an element of novelty about the proceedings, quite irrespective of the actual nature of the intervention. For the experimental group, this possibility makes follow-up important. It may also account for unexpected gains in the control group.

Another possible source of embarrassment is the John Henry effect, when the control group, alerted to the fact that somebody considers them to be in need but is not providing anything for them, consciously determines to improve anyway, and does so without apparent outside intervention.

Types of evaluation

There are two main types of evaluation, summative (or outcome or product) and formative (or process). Summative evaluation looks solely at the end-product or outcome of a project, such as gains in reading skills. Formative evaluation looks closely at how effective each of the various aspects of the organization and methods of the project were in achieving this goal (for example, training quality, attendance rates, technique compliance). Formative evaluation enables you to re-form a better project next time, or even adjust the current one as you go along.

Formative evaluation data can include plans on the PR Planning Proforma (checked against subsequent reality), collected observations on the PR Technique Checklist, and collected PR Diaries (see TRW website). It could include any other observations and opinions collected from participants about the project as you go along. An independent observer to record observations can be very helpful, but this takes time and resources. The effect of the presence of the observer, especially in small group settings, also has to be taken into account.

The section on Measures (below) inevitably focusses mainly on project end-products, although some of the methods discussed throw some tangential light on processes involved.

Measures

There are various basic requirements of any measures you use. Economy of cost in materials and time in administration and scoring are two obvious considerations. The measure needs to be reliable, in the sense of not being susceptible to wild random fluctuations or erratic guesswork. It also needs to be valid, that is it must actually measure what it is purporting to measure. Of equal importance, it needs to be relevant to the processes in question. Thus a phonic skills teaching program would probably not be relevantly evaluated by application of a reading test containing a very high proportion of irregular sight words.

Last, but by no means least, the measure must generate information which is analysable. A vast quantity of impressionistic opinion or observation may be fascinating to the project organizers, but will not enable them to communicate their findings to others in a brief, clear and credible way. These considerations are worth bearing in mind irrespective of the type(s) of measure chosen.

Individual vs. group tests

Reading tests administered individually may give a more valid indication of how well a child can actually read unless they are very brief or the content is restricted to a single narrow kind of reading with very limited context. Reading to a real person sitting with you is also much more like the Paired Reading experience. Even if one child does not respond well and seems inattentive and unmotivated, at least you can observe this and interpret the results accordingly. However, administering one individual test after the other takes far more time than administering a group test.

Group tests are much quicker to administer (although you still have to find time to score each one), but even though you will carefully watch the group of children during testing, you will be much less certain whether scores really reflect the children's reading ability. You must be especially careful about giving individual results on group tests to parents or students. Individual scores may fluctuate implausibly, even though the group averages seem about right.

This dilemma of choice seems likely to be to some extent resolved in well-resourced countries by the increasing introduction of adaptive computer-based assessment of reading skills. This involves each child being tested individually at the computer, with immediate automatic scoring. The test content is adaptively individualized to the child, so testing is brief and stress is limited. Children are generally highly motivated, although the personal interaction element is missing.

Norm-referenced vs. criterion-referenced tests

Some tests are standardized (norm-referenced). This means that the performance of a great many children on the test has been analysed to see what constitutes the normal range of performance for children of specific ages. Each new child's performance can then be compared to these norms. Most such tests have to be purchased.

Curriculum-based or criterion-referenced tests are different. They are used to see whether the child has attained a certain level (criterion) of performance on materials very close to (or maybe drawn from) the curriculum the child is following. If you use such a test with a group of children, you will of course get some idea of what is normal for your group. Some criterion-referenced tests are available commercially, many are available free of charge (increasingly on the Internet), and many are devised by schools or individual teachers for their own purposes.

At first sight, criterion-referenced tests seem more attractive. They are likely to be cheaper and more closely related to what the child has actually done (that is to be evaluated), and probably less likely to frighten or distress weaker students. However, they are more likely only to be available in an individually administered format. Furthermore, information on reliability and validity tends to be much sparser than with standardized tests. Good results on standardized tests may be harder to obtain, but are likely to be more persuasive, because such tests are assessing generalization of improved skills to completely new material and new situations.

Of course, in many countries standardized tests of reading are not available, so criterion-referenced tests are the only option.

Test reliability and validity

The manuals for tests should contain detailed information about their reliability and validity. If this information is inadequate or missing, do not use the test. Even if it is there and reassuringly positive, remember average reliability and validity with a normal distribution of children may not necessarily be the same as the reliability and validity you actually obtain with your small and idiosyncratic group of children.

Where standardized or criterion-referenced tests are in use, pre- and post-project measures should be carried out by the same person, to ensure that peculiarities of administration or any bias (particularly generosity in scoring) or other tester effects will be the same on both occasions.

Test range

If your readers (experimental and control) cover a wide range of reading ability, make sure the test you choose covers this range. Remember that at post-test, performance and chronological age will be higher, and this will be even more true at follow-up. Beware of tests which suffer from a ceiling or floor effect for your purposes (i.e. no discrimination or maybe no scores at all for very able or less able readers, or very young or very old readers). So children with a high pre-test score have little scope to better it, while at the other extreme many children may be given the same very low (or below scale) score when they are actually quite different in reading competence. On the other hand, if the test is very long in order to include many items at all levels of difficulty, it will be very oppressive for the weaker readers, whose self-esteem may be damaged by testing. However, also watch for calibration effects – some tests include many items covering the middle part of the total span they purport to cover, but very few items at the extremes. At the extremes, getting just one more item right or wrong could make a big difference to the standardized performance score.

Test content and aim

Some tests still available were created long ago and have very dated content. Older tests (and some of the newer ones) have a strong cultural bias, often favoring white middle-class children who speak English as their first language. Look for words, events or ideas that might be currently common in some cultural groups but not in others.

As mentioned above, very brief tests and/or those with content restricted to a single narrow kind of reading with very limited context are unlikely to be satisfactory. Look for tests that give a reading experience somewhat like real reading, at least passages of continuous meaningful prose.

Consider if the test is really only measuring accuracy of decoding, or whether it is also assessing comprehension. The latter is highly desirable, of course. Consider whether it can assess comprehension only if decoding accuracy is good. Does it also measure speed or rate of reading? This may not however be very important, since for some children reading slower is actually an improvement.

Test practice effects

If children do better at post-test than at pre-test, might it just be because they have remembered some of the answers, and therefore have more energy to attack the harder items? This is called a 'content practice effect' on a repeat test with the same content. Even if the post-test had different test items, children would be familiar with the format, and might do better owing to that (a format practice effect). Both of these are reasons for using a control group, for whom any practice effects would be the same.

Practice effects are not always positive, however. Children may be bored with the test at second encounter and consequently unmotivated. Or if it is a very long test, and they know they struggled with a majority of the items at first encounter, they may give up completely right from the start.

Where tests are available in parallel forms (to limit content practice effects if not format practice effects), check carefully that the parallel forms are actually equivalent. Sometimes they are not. To guard against this possibility, you can allocate particular test forms to children by occasion: one child has form A at pre-test and form B at post-test, while another child has form B first. This also helps reduce the possibility of copying answers, a potential problem with group test administration in a crowded classroom.

Quality and recency of standardization

Producing good standardized tests is expensive. In too many cases, test standardization suffers from being highly localized. Check if the samples used for the standardization really represent the whole country. Are they likely to represent your students? Some of the tests currently in use were standardized many years ago. Look for a relatively recent standardization or re-standardization, perhaps in a new edition.

Informal reading inventories

An Informal Reading Inventory is a kind of curriculum-based test. It is based on a series of passages of increasing difficulty taken from typical reading material in the real life context, carefully graded for difficulty, with associated comprehension questions. Readability can be assessed through one of the standard formulas (now available as computer programs for scanned text), or the passages could be systematically drawn from some pre-leveled material such as basal readers or a reading scheme. Children are asked to read the passages in order of increasing difficulty until they reach their frustration level. The independence level is defined as 99 per cent Accuracy and 90 per cent Comprehension; Instructional Level as 95 per cent Accuracy and 75 per cent Comprehension; Frustration Level as 90 per cent (or less) Accuracy and 50 per cent (or less) Comprehension.

While the student is reading, a practiced tester can also note the nature of the errors made, allowing subsequent diagnostic error analysis (miscue analysis). Unfortunately IRIs are time-consuming to devise and individually administer. However, they are much more like real reading. The results of a Paired Reading project evaluated by an IRI would not, of course, be readily comparable to those of another school using an IRI based on a different curriculum or reading scheme.

Cloze tests

An alternative is a Cloze test, again based on curriculum materials in a sequence of ascending difficulty. A series of passages are reproduced with some words deleted. The deletions can be predominantly syntactic or semantic, a combination of both, or random. The children have to supply the missing words. If the exercise is done on a silent reading basis, which is the more common, no emphasis is placed on spelling correctness in the child's insertions. The disadvantages of IRIs are shared by Cloze tests. Cloze tests on a silent reading basis involve less actual time expenditure by the tester, but yield less useful information. Some commercial standardized tests use a Cloze structure.

High frequency words

Especially with young, emergent or delayed readers, finding any test with a low enough floor and sufficient discrimination to register any improvement may be difficult. One possibility is to construct a word recognition test from the Dolch or Edwards or more recent lists of the most commonly occurring (high frequency) words. Much the same exercise can be carried out using items of vocabulary from the school's core basal reading scheme. Scoring can be in terms of number of words read correctly out of a given set of words, or in terms of how many words the child can read correctly in a given time. There are different views about whether reading faster is necessarily a good thing, but speeded tests may be worth a try as a measure of fluency on vocabulary which should be familiar. Of course, how reading isolated words relates to the contextualized reading that characterizes the PR process is questionable. With such groups, assessments of developing awareness of the reading process (such as Clay's Concepts about Print or Downing's Linguistic Awareness in Reading Readiness scale) may also be worthwhile.

Attitude to reading

A variety of Attitude to Reading scales is available, but many are long and complex paper and pencil exercises of doubtful relevance and limited specificity, quite apart from the considerations of reliability and validity. The Elementary Reading Attitude Survey (McKenna and Kear, 1990, 1995) uses a Garfield cartoon character which appeals to young children. Also in the public domain is the Motivation To Read Profile (Gambrell *et al.*, 1996).

Self-concept scales

The socio-emotional aspects of Paired Reading are highly significant, and attempts can be made to tap these by some form of measure. Some group tests of self-concept are available, and in some cases these are sub-divided into academic self-concept and other areas of self-concept. Single tests specifically of reading self-concept are rare, but the Reader Self-Perception Scale (Henk and Melnick, 1995) is available in the public domain. The very complexity and intangibility of the socio-emotional factors involved render them difficult to reveal on paper and pencil measures.

Subjective feedback

The subjective views of the major participants in the project (tutees, parent tutors, peer tutors, volunteer tutors, teachers) should always be elicited in some way. To rely simply on primitive instruments such as tests is to risk missing the texture of the reality of what happened. The participants will probably offer more process insights than summative conclusions, but the former must not be neglected. Formulating and communicating opinions serves not only to gather information, but also to clarify the participant's views on the subject, resolve any residual practical problems, and very often to recharge and commit the participants to continued effort.

A group meeting for all participants at the end of the initial period is a good idea. This could be tape-recorded (audio or video) for more detailed analysis later (although such analysis can prove a massive task). If time is available, individual interviews with at least the parents along a semi-structured format is desirable, (perhaps in the context of the last home visit if these are taking place). Similar interviews with the children and teachers are desirable, but probably need carrying out by an outsider to the project if they are to be remotely objective.

Realistically, time constraints and/or the need to have readily analysable data often drive people into using some form of structured questionnaire. However, there are very large doubts about the reliability and validity of questionnaires, even supposing you obtain a high response rate. Other forms of data gathering should be carried out as well. The kind of superficial subjective feedback gathered by questionnaires may be particularly susceptible to the grateful testimonials effect. Your respondents know you have worked hard, think you are a nice person, and do not want to tell you anything except what they think you want to hear. If the response rate to your questionnaire is low, it is even more likely that the returns will be biased positively.

In the construction of questionnaires, the project leaders or participants are best placed to decide which questions are important. However, they must be structured to eliminate any possibility of leading respondents into giving a particular answer. A multiple choice format gives easily analysable data but is crude and simplistic, while an open-ended format is dependent on the free writing skills of the respondents and yields data which is often difficult to analyse. Where a self-designed questionnaire is used, you should pilot it with a relevant sub-group in your own locality first.

If you want people's feelings about the project, ask for them directly, but do not expect them to necessarily bear much relationship to the participants' actual behavior or even the children's progress in reading. On the other hand, if you want observations of what participants actually did, ask for that directly, giving a 'no observations made' option. But avoid confusing the two.

Specimen PR Evaluation Questionnaires will be found on the TRW website. These include questionnaires for parent tutors, for peer tutors, for tutees (irrespective of tutor), and for teachers or other project organizers (with respect to individual children or the whole class/group). These have the advantage of previous widespread use, at least in the UK The results can be considered to form a crude kind of standardization or norm-reference (see Topping and Whiteley, 1990).

These have been carefully constructed to avoid leading the respondents into 'yea-saying'. Thus, even if you feel the exact questions are not relevant to your context, you may wish to reflect upon the structure. If you are able to conduct individual interviews, specimen interview schedules for Paired Writing are available on the TRW website, which should give you ideas for a Paired Reading interview schedule.

Analysis of data

There is a great difference between statistical and educational significance. The larger your sample, the more likely you are to obtain statistical significance, other things being equal. Big gains for your Paired Readers compared to a control group may not be statistically significant if you have only five children in each group. On the other hand, if a very large Paired Reading project produces gains in the project group which compared to those in the control group are only just statistically significant at the 5 per cent probability level, searching questions need to be asked about the educational significance of the results. Was it worth all that time and effort for gains so small?

It should also be borne in mind that where a large number of different outcome measures are used, the chances are that one or two will show statistically significant changes irrespective of any real impact of the project (with the attendant risk of assuming the intervention has worked when in fact it has not, a Type 1 error). Fortunately, Paired Reading projects do not usually find themselves in this area of doubt, since the majority of moderately well organized Paired Reading projects show gains of at least twice normal rates of progress during the project, and the educational significance of this is rarely in doubt, even before more subjective feedback is considered.

For those unsure of their competence in statistical analysis, or doubting the validity of the procedures, simple comparison of raw data on scattergrams or graphing of shifts in averages for groups gives a ready visual indication of changes. Certainly the data is worth summarizing in this way for feedback to the participants, who may be assumed to be statistically unsophisticated.

If you really want to do some statistical analysis, you need to consider:

- the level of measurement of your measures
- the size of your samples
- the nature of your sampling framework
- the nature of the comparisons you wish to make (within or between groups)

before you can decide whether to use parametric or non-parametric statistical analysis. Consult a statistics textbook or one of the public domain on-line Internet tutorials (a web search engine will find the current ones). If you do not understand what the things are you need to consider, you definitely need to consult a statistics textbook.

Evaluation results feedback

One of the disadvantages of complex data analysis is that it takes time, and very often early feedback of evaluation results to the project participants is highly desirable, to renew their commitment and recharge their energies. A simple graph and/or brief tables of average scores for the groups is probably the best vehicle for this. Remember, the results must be understood by the children as well.

The unreliability of group tests makes giving individual test scores to individual families a risky business, and care must be taken throughout not to give undue emphasis to standardized test data as distinct from other types. Individual test scores are best given in an individual interview rather than at a group meeting, if given at all.

In any event it is best for one person to take the responsibility for collating and presenting the evaluation data, or it may lie about on scraps of paper forever. Evaluation results have a number of other uses as well. Publicity via the local press, professional journals, education curriculum bulletins or in-service meetings not only helps to disseminate good practice and help more children, it also serves to boost the morale of the project initiators and participants.

The results may be useful to convince skeptics on the school staff, generate a wider interest and produce a more coherent future policy on parent involvement in the school. The school board of governors or parents' council will be interested, as should be various district or state officers. A demonstration of cost-effectiveness may elicit more tangible support from administrators and politicians. Associated services such as children's library services, and reading and language centers may be drawn into the network of community support by a convincing evaluation report.

So to the final word. If you get results you don't like, you'll spend hours puzzling over them trying to explain them away. Make sure that if you get results you do like, you spend as much time and energy searching for other factors outside the project that could have produced them. If you don't spot them, someone else may – and probably will!

Part Two

Paired Thinking

6 What Is Paired Thinking?

> Readers are plentiful: thinkers are rare.
> *Harriet Martineau*

> There is more to be learned from the unexpected questions of
> children than the discourses of men.   *John Locke*

> There ain't no answer. There ain't going to be any answer.
> There never has been an answer. That's the answer.
> *Gertrude Stein*

Intellectual skills are acquired in many and various ways (Voss *et al.*,
1995). There has been great interest in the actual direct teaching of
thinking skills in recent years. However, the general picture in the
research literature is of more activity of this kind in colleges and
universities than in high schools, and more activity in high schools
than in elementary schools.

The reports in the research literature are of three broad types:

1. Teaching thinking skills embedded in one or more traditional curriculum subjects (e.g. social studies, physical
   science).
2. Teaching thinking skills embedded in or linked to another
   broadly applicable transferable skill, such as reading, writing, or research skills.
3. Teaching thinking skills as a largely abstract free-standing
   activity, using de-contextualized tasks or games.

There is considerable debate about the relative merits of these different approaches (Powell, 1987; Nickerson, 1988; Nisbet and Davies,
1990).

Teaching thinking skills embedded in curriculum subjects (the
infusion approach) may be motivating and make sense to the stu-

dents, but will the thinking skills developed in this situation automatically generalize to other subjects and situations?

On the other hand, teaching thinking skills as a largely abstract free-standing activity (the add-on approach) requires the teacher to find more time in a crowded curriculum schedule, and raises even larger questions about whether the skills will automatically generalize to curriculum subjects or other situations, tasks and contexts.

Students who have learned to do intelligence games competently, but still act dumb in other aspects of their lives, have not made a giant leap for humankind. In a meta-analysis of twenty controlled studies of instruction for critical thinking, Bangert-Drowns and Bankert (1990) found that methods involving explicit instruction that addressed generalization issues yielded the highest effect sizes.

Virtually all the research literature is concerned with teacher-directed instruction in thinking skills. Very little is concerned with peer tutoring (with a few notable exceptions, discussed below). There is practically no literature on parent or volunteer tutoring.

Thus it seems that the Paired Thinking method stands to make a significant original contribution to research and practice.

Thinking embedded in a subject

A good example of this approach is the CASE (Cognitive Acceleration through Science Education) program of Adey and Shayer (1994). CASE was designed to promote 'thinking science' in high school. Thirty specimen lessons were designed, intended to be interspersed with regular science lessons. Evaluation involved Piagetian reasoning tasks at pre-test, post-test and follow-up, coupled with performance on national examinations. The Piagetian tasks showed significant gains overall, albeit with considerable variance. The national examinations gave a general picture of CASE/control differences being sustained to follow-up, to the extent of two thirds of a standard deviation, although data were missing for some groups.

Perkins and Grotzer (1997) reviewed studies designed to teach students to be more able thinkers in particular subject areas. History, social studies, psychology and many other subjects feature.

Thinking linked to other transferable skills

The early work of Louis Raths and his colleagues (1967) offered an elaborated typology of questioning, which could be used by teachers in virtually any subject, as well as a typology of thinking styles. A review of 26 studies of teaching students to generate questions as a means of improving their comprehension and thinking skills was conducted by Rosenshine *et al.* (1996). Overall, modest effect scores in terms of outcomes on standardized tests were balanced by substantial effect scores on criterion-referenced assessments. The authors include a helpful analysis of the pedagogical elements of the interventions evaluated.

Pressley and Woloshyn (1995) reported a number of evidence-based methods for cognitive strategy instruction, applicable to a range of basic skills in elementary schools. Related books include Mayfield's (1987) *Thinking for Yourself: Developing Critical Thinking Skills Through Writing* and Rosenberg's (1989) *Reading, Writing and Thinking: Critical Connections*. The issue of peer interaction in teaching reading and thinking skills has been addressed generally by Gambrell and Alamasi (1996) in *Lively Discussions! Fostering Engaged Reading*; by Beck, McKeown, Hamilton and Kucan (1997) in *Questioning The Author: Student Engagement with Text*; and by Paratore and McCormack (1997) in *Peer Talk in the Classroom*.

Diane Halpern (1998) addressed the issues involved in teaching critical thinking to transfer across domains, and from institutions of learning into the workplace. She proposed a four-part model for teaching and learning thinking skills. The first of these is a dispositional component to prepare learners for the effort of cognitive challenge. In addition to thinking skills instruction, Halpern argued that learners need specific training in the generalization of those skills, and training in methods to continuously check and evaluate the quality and effectiveness of their onward application of the skills.

In the UK, Coles and Robinson (1991) conducted a survey of a large number of programs for teaching thinking, summarizing the explosion in the field in recent years. McGuinness (1999) reviewed the effectiveness of approaches for developing the thinking of school students, concluding that the teaching of thinking skills as a scheduled activity was less effective than the creation of the thinking classroom.

Within a workplace environment, the definition of thinking skills changes focus, and is more likely to include attention allocation, self-regulation, transfer of training, task analysis and instructional design as well as problem-solving (Redding [1990] reviewed this literature). Several clinical professions such as nursing now include a thinking skills component in training.

Paired Thinking takes this middle approach, embedding thinking skills in the very broadly applicable transferable skill of reading. Thus it is intended to provide a framework for the infusion of thinking skills through all curriculum subjects and all activities in which reading is involved.

Thinking as abstract activity

Philosophy for Children (Lipman, 1984) aims to strengthen children's powers of reasoning and moral judgment through Socratic dialog and other forms of discussion, intended to sharpen conceptual definition and analysis. Students bring any issues of interest to them into the dialog. In addition to studies conducted by Lipman, there is some independent evidence of increased achievement in traditional subjects as well as reasoning, and of improvement in personal and interpersonal skills (Lim, 1995; Niklasson *et al.*, 1996; Garcia-Moriyon, Colom *et al.*, 2000). In the UK, the related work of Fisher (1990) is popular.

DeBono's work on lateral thinking is well known (e.g. DeBono, 1990). His CoRT program of 60 thinking skills lessons for students aged 12 years or more is also long-established, but there is limited evidence of consistent gains, particularly of transfer to curriculum subjects.

Reuven Feuerstein's Instrumental Enrichment (IE) program consists of thirteen sections, each containing between one and 24 activities, to be taught for five hours each week for two years. It involves a general problem-solving model, including the stages of input, elaboration and output. An evaluation study indicated modest effect sizes on an intelligence test, with little significant transfer to performance in school subjects. However, there was evidence of greater differences at long-term follow-up (Rand *et al.*, 1981). Carl Haywood at Vanderbilt University subsequently reported substantial effect sizes for IE on abstract tests, but again limited generalization to school subjects. He later developed his own variant program for younger children, Bright Start. The empirical research on IE was reviewed by Savell *et al.* (1986), and by Shayer and Beasley (1987), suggesting that the evidence for generalized effects was tentative, and questioning cost-effectiveness. Blagg (1991) evaluated the impact of IE in the one large school district in the UK using multiple outcome measures, but found no differences between experimental and control students on any measure, although there were questions about implementation integrity.

Teaching of reading and thinking skills

Embedding the teaching of thinking skills in the transferable skill of reading has the advantage that reading is probably the most used means of obtaining information that requires deep processing, despite the competing claims of listening comprehension and visual comprehension. It is unclear where the borderline might be between thinking skills and higher order reading skills that focus on deep comprehension, but perhaps it does not matter.

Probably the most widely known reading and thinking method is SQ3R:

- Survey (title, pictures and other structural features of the book)
- Question (develop a question about each chapter)
- Read
- Recite (provisional answers to the questions)
- Review (check).

The strategies were first described under this acronym by Francis Robinson around 1946, and have thus been in use for over a half-century. However, the ideas were not new even then, and can be traced back at least as far as 1924.

Reviews of studies of the effectiveness of SQ3R (Kopfstein, 1982; Gustafson and Pederson, 1985) have found generally positive but somewhat mixed results, with SQ3R sometimes found to be no better than simpler procedures such as underlining key words. However, the method has been implemented in various ways, sometimes only sketchily described in reports, so making overall conclusions is difficult. Details of training procedures were often insufficient to enable exact replication, and most of the studies were conducted with college students. Additionally, evidence on generalization to other reading across the curriculum and out of school is very hard to find, as is evidence on maintenance of effects over longer time periods.

SQ3R spawned sundry adaptations, such as R3SW (Read, Search, Select, Study, Write), PQ4R (Preview, Question, Read, Reflect, Recite, Review), SQ5R (Survey, Question, Record, Reduce, Recite, Reflect, Review) and even SQ10R. A tidal wave of acronymic adaptations followed, including K-W-L (what do we Know? what do we Want to know? what have we Learned?), RARE (Review, Answer, Read, Express), PORPE (Predict, Organize, Rehearse, Practice, Evaluate), RESPONSE, LETME, ReQUEST, PReP, REAP and MURDER, as well as the more prosaically named Multipass and Structured Comprehension. However, evaluation evidence tends to be even more limited.

In the early 1980s, Taffy Raphael (1986) developed her QAR approach: Question–Answer–Relationships. In four training sessions, children learned to use four kinds of self-questions: Right There (literal detail in immediate text), Think and Search (interpretative/inferential), On My Own (critical and evaluative), and Author and Me. However, subsequent evaluation research was limited.

At about the same time the Reciprocal Teaching method was developed by Palincsar and Brown (1988), with Prediction, Questioning, Summarizing and Clarifying as the key strategies. Rosenshine and Meister (1994) later published an excellent review of sixteen quantitative studies of reciprocal teaching, which generally supported the efficacy of this method.

A number of other approaches with rather similar labels arrived over the years: Directed Reading Activity (DRA), Directed Reading and Thinking Activity (DRTA), and Directed Activities in Relation to Texts (DARTS). These were all strongly teacher-controlled, with more or less standardized questions issued by the teacher for specified books. DRTA emphasized prediction and verification (Haggard, 1988). DARTS focussed on key words, labeling, extracting, and assembly – i.e. text analysis and reconstruction (Davies and

Greene, 1981). Again, research on outcomes is of variable quality and rather limited.

Yuill and Oakhill (1988) developed Inference Awareness Training, requiring children to make inferences, generate questions and check comprehension. Outcomes were positive with small numbers of lower ability children, but no better than from more traditional comprehension exercises.

Block (1993) evaluated a program to teach critical reading and thinking strategies through a student-centered literature-based curriculum. Experimental students (n = 178) significantly outperformed 174 controls on standardized tests of reading comprehension, assessments of critical and creative thinking, and ability to transfer cognitive strategies outside of school.

Transactional Strategies Instruction (Brown *et al.*, 1996) is a year-long program that instructs students in specific strategies to guide problem-solving when experiencing a failure of comprehension. (The program seems to require high levels of meta-ignorance in the students – the ability to know that they do not know.) The program has proved effective in raising scores on standardized measures of reading comprehension with low-achieving children in second grade, in comparison to distal control groups.

Over the years, many of these methods have included different constellations of a similar or common core of strategies. Prediction, Questioning and Summarizing are particularly common features. However, almost all the methods have been mainly delivered directly by professional teachers.

Peer tutoring of reading and thinking skills

Collaborative learning has long been considered useful in the development of thinking skills (e.g. Nelson, 1994, who emphasizes the importance of both cognitive structuring and role structuring). Reading comprehension strategy instruction and cooperative small group learning were blended in Collaborative Strategic Reading (Klingner and Vaughn, 1999), and demonstrated effectiveness in at least one controlled study. However, extending this into paired peer tutoring, with more precise specification of interactive behavior, is relatively rare.

One early example was that of Sindelar (1982) in the US, who operated cross-age tutoring based on the Hypothesis-Test procedure of
Samuels. Results indicated gains as good as a comparison group
taught by professional teachers using the same method, although
the experimental children did show their best gains on a Cloze measure which was similar to Cloze materials used within the project
activities.

In New Zealand, Pickens and McNaughton (1988) reported same-
age peer tutoring of simple comprehension strategies with low
achieving eleven- to twelve-year-olds. Tutors were only six months
more able in reading comprehension than tutees. Positive results
were again found on Cloze measures, but the numbers involved were
small.

Bowers (1991) described the use of peer tutoring in second and
third grade with at-risk students, who applied critical thinking skills
to reading activities, 30 minutes each day for twelve weeks. The
tutees improved from scores at the 35th percentile (on average) to
post-test scores of 95 per cent, but no control group was assessed.

In Holland, the Stap Door program was designed specifically for
peer (and parent) tutoring (Fukkink *et al.*, 1997). With respect to reading comprehension, it has five key strategy components: activating
prior knowledge, word study, predicting, checking understanding
and identifying main ideas. However, the program is heavily dependent on structured reading materials (available only in Dutch), and
the evaluation results currently available do not indicate the specific
impact of the comprehension strategy components.

The PALS (Peer Assisted Learning Strategies) program integrates
comprehension strategies (including re-telling, summarizing, predicting and elaborated help-giving) within class-wide peer tutoring.
In a series of studies by Fuchs and Fuchs and their colleagues, PALS
students were found to make greater gains in reading comprehension than controls, although elaborated help-giving proved more
effective with older students (Simmons *et al.*, 1994; Fuchs *et al.*, 1999).

Margo Mastropieri and Tom Scruggs (2000) deployed reciprocal
peer tutoring in comprehension strategies with middle school students with learning disabilities. There was a strong emphasis on summarization activity. Performance on reading comprehension tests
showed significant advantages for students involved in tutoring,

compared to a traditional reading instruction condition.

King (1999) offers a useful overview of her approach, which essentially involves scaffolding discourse patterns through guided peer questioning. Structured question stems are used to promote analytic and critical discourse in dyads and in small groups, at three levels of complexity. In a controlled study the program has been shown to improve the solving of novel problems. King (1997) developed the 'Ask To Think – Tel Why' (sic) peer tutoring model, involving several types of questions (to review, elaborate, build, probe, hint, solicit meta-cognition, and so on). King *et al.* (1998) involved 58 seventh graders in peer tutoring. The same-age, same-ability, same-sex dyads successfully reciprocally scaffolded higher order thinking and learning. The trained discourse pattern was quite different from naturalistic untrained tutorial dialogue patterns. Relatedly, O'Donnell (1999) discusses Danserau's even more structured scripted cooperation procedures.

The relatively few studies of peer tutoring in thinking skills have generally reported encouraging results. This is in contrast to the teacher-directed methods that hitherto have been much more widely used, but generally poorly evaluated (with some notable exceptions).

Paired Thinking has strong links with King's work, in that it provides questions as cues to scaffold analytic and critical discourse between pairs. It differs from King's work in that it specifically builds that discourse on a reading experience chosen and shared by the pair.

Aims and design parameters for Paired Thinking

Given these many different approaches, yet another elaborate and idiosyncratic method is probably the last thing a busy teacher needs. Therefore, Paired Thinking (PT) seeks to distil many of the most important features of previous methods into a practical and flexible package which can be easily used in diverse classrooms. It does this by developing children's ability to ask each other intelligent questions about what they have read together.

The design of PT deliberately incorporates many of the positive features of Paired Reading.

Paired Thinking provides:

- modeling of intelligent questioning by the tutor
- interactive cognitive challenge for both partners
- practice in critical and analytic thinking
- scaffolding
- feedback
- praise and other social reinforcement.

Paired Thinking also:

- applies flexibly to any reading experience shared by the pair
- enables the pair to pursue their own interests and motivations
- is highly adapted to the individual learner's needs of the moment
- is democratic and encourages learner-managed learning
- encourages critical and analytic discussion in the pair's vernacular vocabulary
- encourages self-disclosure of faulty or deficient thinking.

Paired Thinking includes reading, listening, thinking, feeling and communicating. It also aims to help pupils to identify, review and evaluate the values they and others hold, and recognize how these affect thoughts and actions.

The Structure of Paired Thinking

Paired Thinking has three stages (before, during and after reading).

The three stages encompass thirteen activities (dealing with structure, type, difficulty, reader aims, author aims, meaning, truth, prediction, links, summarize, evaluate, revisit, extend).

The thirteen activities are supported by prompt sheets of questions. These are available in four differentiated levels of complexity and difficulty to suit different pairs and provide some developmental progression. The most complex level (4) has 21 sub-categories.

Additionally, there are 21 Tips for Tutors, available as a brief reminder sheet and with a fuller explanation.

The structure of the thirteen activities in the three stages is outlined below, together with some sample questions for each activity.

Stage 1: Before reading
(priming)

Structure	'What do the parts of the book tell us?'
Type	'What kind of book is it?'
Difficulty	'How hard is it?'
Reader Aims	'What do you want from the book?'

Stage 2: During reading
(formative)

Author Aims	'What does the writer want?'
Meaning	'What does it mean?'
Truth	'Is it true?'
Prediction	'What might happen next?'
Links	'What does it remind us of?'

Stage 3: After reading
(formative and summative)

Summarize	'What are the main ideas?'
Evaluate	'How do you feel about it?'
Revisit	'What did you remember about it?'
Extend	'Have you questioned anything else?'

This is the whole content of the Level 1 question prompt sheet (see TRW website). For the training sessions and for subsequent regular sessions, all pairs start with a Level 1 prompt sheet.

The interactive behavior required is outlined in the Tips for Tutors handout. Main points from this are summarized below. These are abbreviated for everyday use in the Tips for Tutors Reminder Sheet (see TRW website). When initially presenting them to pairs, teachers often present just a few at a time, and not necessarily in this order.

Interactive behavior: Tips for Tutors

- Your aim is to improve the tutee's quality of thinking by asking helpful and intelligent questions which give clues. This is not as easy as you might think!

- Tutors have to think hard, too – they do not just work through a list of given questions.

- You need to put tutees at their ease, boost their confidence, and encourage them to trust you – or they will be afraid to let you know what they are thinking.

- During reading, pause quite often at any natural break in the reading to think and talk about what you have read.

- Remember tutees are not as old as you and don't know as much as you do, so don't expect too much or push them too hard.

- Encourage tutees to 'think aloud', so you can hear HOW they are thinking and really understand them – if they think alone then just give you their final answer, you will not understand how they got there.

- You might 'think aloud' yourself sometimes, to show them how to do it.

- Sometimes you can also try to 'brainstorm' answers – this is where both of you say every possible answer that comes into your head, even if it seems silly or weird. Then choose the best.

- Never say 'No' or 'That's wrong' – always ask another question to give a clue.

- Although there are many questions, it is not a 'test' for the tutee. Indeed, often there is no one 'right' answer, only many 'better' or 'worse' answers. Work toward getting more 'better' answers. But even the tutor need not know the answer to the question at the beginning – you can work it out together.

- Tutees can ask tutors questions, too! Keep each other thinking!

- It's OK for both tutors and tutees to say they 'don't know' – but be clear about what you need to know and think about how you might find out.

- Give the tutees some time to think – they will not usually be able to answer straight away. But if they think for more than half a minute without success, maybe they need a clue in another question.

- Praise the tutee for all thoughtful responses – for example: 'Good, I can tell you thought hard about that'.

- The questions listed are only examples to get you started – please do think up your own questions as well. Your own questions should encourage the tutee to say whatever they really think, not push them towards one 'right answer'.

- Tutors can say what they think, too – but be careful not let tutees assume that must be the 'right answer' – ask the tutee what they think as well.

- You might need to go back to read bits of the book again at any time to check on things or answer questions. When you do, you might want to read the difficult bit to the tutee, so they can think about it.

- Some of the listed questions apply only to story books, some apply only to information books. Just leave out the questions which don't apply to the book you are reading.

- When you are stuck trying to think of a question quickly, 'How do you know that?' is often a good one.

- When you are reading a longer book, you might find the tutee has trouble remembering everything, even if they did understand it in the first place. If they don't remember, it does not always mean they never did understand.

- You might find tutees remember the beginning or end of a book better than the middle – but they do need to think about the middle as well!

- In the 'During Reading' Stage, the five Activities (Author Aims, Meaning, Truth, Prediction, Links) can be worked through in any order. Choose any relevant questions from any Activity at any time.

- In the 'After Reading' Stage when you are finding the main ideas or 'Summarizing', and choose to write down some key-words and/or write a summary for your classmates, it is usually easier if the tutor does any writing – but the tutor must not do all the thinking!

- In the 'After Reading' Stage when you are doing 'Self-Assessment', this is a good time to really praise each other – AGAIN!

Differentiation and progression: levels of prompt sheet

As pairs progress at different rates in subsequent sessions, Level 2, 3 and 4 prompt sheets can be issued to particular pairs as you judge appropriate. Level 2 is intended to be a relatively small step from Level 1 (to encourage all concerned), so all pairs should eventually progress to Level 2. However, progression to Levels 3 and 4 will be much more dependent upon the abilities of individual pairs.

The levels are intended to enable the project organizer to differentiate and individualize the thinking activities for different pairs progressively, adding layers of complexity and sophistication, without making too much work.

To exemplify this progression, it is worth comparing the prompt questions at each level for two of the Activities: Prediction and Summarize (see below). The complete prompt sheets for all four levels are on the TRW website.

Prediction

Level 1
'What might happen next?'

Level 2
'What might happen next?' (Prediction)

- What do you think might happen next?
- What might make this happen? How likely is this?
- Can you imagine or picture in your head what it would look like?
- Did the book end as you expected? How else might it have ended?

Level 3
'What might happen next?' (Prediction)

- What do the people in the book want or expect to happen next?
- What have you learnt about them which helps you to guess what they might do next?

- What do you think might happen next?
- How likely is this?
- What might cause this to happen?
- Might it depend on something else happening? What?
- Can you imagine or picture in your head what it would look like?
- Did the book end or conclude as you expected?
- How else might it have ended?

Level 4
'What might happen next?' (Prediction, Inference and Deduction)

- What do the people in the book want or expect to happen next? (Intentionality)
- What have you learnt about them which helps you to guess what they might do next? (Characterization)
- What do you think might happen next? (Prediction)
- How likely is this? (Probability, Uncertainty)
- What might cause this to happen? (Causality)
- One cause or more? (Multiple, Complex, Interdependent Causality)
- How would you know what had really caused it? (Evidence)
- Might it depend on something else happening? What? (Conditionality)
- Will it only happen if something else happens?
- One thing or more than one? (Multiple, Complex, Interdependent Conditionality)
- Might there be a biggest or major cause? (Critical Factor or Incident)
- If this doesn't happen, what else might? (Alternatives)
- Can you imagine or picture in your head what it would look like? (Visual Imagery)
- Did the book end or conclude as you expected?
- How else might it have ended?

Summarize

Level 1
'What are the main ideas?'

Level 2
'What are the main ideas?' (Summarize)

- What were the most important points to you?
- Can we make a list or map or chart of the main ideas, to help us?
- Can we tell another pair the most important points?
- Can we think up some questions to make a quiz for other pairs?

Level 3
'What are the main ideas?' (Summarize)

Find Main Ideas

- What were the most important points to you?
- What were some key words?
- Do we need to read any bits again?

Clarify Main Ideas

- Can you say the most important points of the book more clearly?

Sequence Main Ideas

- Do we have the most important points in the best order?
- Can we make a map or chart of the main ideas to help us?

Re-Tell Main Ideas

- Can we tell another pair the most important points?
- Or should we write it down for the whole class?

Quiz on Main Ideas

- Can we think up some questions about the most important points to make a quiz for other pairs?
- Can we write it down for the whole class?

Level 4
'What are the main ideas?' (Summarize)

Find Main Ideas (Focus, Prioritize)

- Who?, Do?, What?, Where?, Why?, To?, How?, With?, Then?
- What were the most important points to you?
- What were some key words?
- Do we need to read any bits again?

Clarify Main Ideas (Reformulation, Reconstruction)

- Can you say the most important points of the book more clearly?

Sequence Main Ideas (Reformulation, Reconstruction)

- Do we have the most important points in the best order?
- Can we make a map or chart of the main ideas to help us?

Re-Tell Main Ideas (Communicate)

- Can we tell another pair the most important points?
- Or should we write it down for the whole class?
- Should we read our writing to each other before we give it to anybody else?

Quiz on Main Ideas (Interrogate)

- Can we think up some questions about the most important points to make a quiz for other pairs?
- Can we write it down for the whole class?

- Should we read it to each other before we give it to anybody else?

Level 4 is obviously elaborate and over-inclusive – indeed perhaps better suited to high school or even college students. However, some very able elementary school students may prove able to handle it.

You may want to look over the whole of the prompt sheets for all levels at this time (on the TRW website).

How these materials are used in practice is explored further in the next chapter.

7 How To Organize Paired Thinking

Paired Thinking projects follow many of the organizational guidelines for Paired Reading projects (reading Chapter 3 before this chapter will be helpful).

You will be able to use much of the PR parent and peer tutoring Planning Proformas (see TRW website) in planning a Paired Thinking project. Similar organizational questions must be answered about context and objectives, recruitment, selection and matching, training, organization of contact, support and monitoring, feedback, and evaluation. One planning area which is very different is, of course, materials. In what follows, repetition will be avoided as far as possible, emphasis being given to significant organizational differences for Paired Thinking as compared to PR.

Parent or peer or volunteer tutoring?

The context and objectives for your Paired Thinking project should be considered and specified, much as you would for Paired Reading. At the time of writing (late 2000), Paired Thinking had been extensively used in peer tutoring, and a major project to develop the method with parents and children at home was about to start. Consequently, clear advice based on practical experience can be given about Paired Thinking with peer tutors, and this is the main emphasis of this chapter. Guidelines about involving parents and volunteers in Paired Thinking will have to be extrapolated from this and the PR guidelines, until practical experience with such tutors has accumulated (updates will be posted on the TRW website).

Interface with Paired Reading

Many schools have chosen to operate Paired Thinking projects to follow directly on from Paired Reading projects with the same groups of tutors and tutees (although not necessarily the same pairings). There are great advantages in this in situations where the tutors and tutees were previously uncertain about how to read together effectively.

Paired Reading is an excellent method for getting tutors and tutees into a successful joint learning experience, including learning to take turns, praise, adapt to each other's idiosyncrasies, personality and learning style, and cooperate in other ways. It gives a solid foundation on which to build the more complex and challenging activities of Paired Thinking.

However, for some pairs there is a paradoxical down side. Some pairs enjoy Paired Reading so much, that they want to go on doing PR and not bother with the Paired Thinking component. Paired Thinking is more intellectually challenging for both tutor and tutee (but particularly the tutor) – it is harder work. Also, it is more interruptive (the tutor interjects frequently) and it feels less like a 'flow' experience than PR.

Given this, you may choose to condition the expectations of the participants from the outset for a two-phase project – Paired Reading then Paired Thinking. After the PR training, allow PR practice to continue for only a few sessions, long enough for you to be satisfied all pairs have reached some minimum level of competence with the method. Then introduce Paired Thinking training, before the participants have become too comfortable with Paired Reading by itself.

In subsequent sessions, you may allow one pure Paired Reading session per week for those who want it, provided there is also one intense Paired Thinking session per week. You will understand the mentality and sociology of your own students best, and manage the project accordingly.

Why do the pair have to actually read the book together? With some organizational changes, this may not be necessary.

Remember that Paired Reading is a cross-ability method – the tutor has to be a somewhat more able reader than the tutee. This has the advantage that the tutee is enabled to access more challenging books. However, you could also try operating Paired Thinking in same-ability pairs, requiring each pair to agree on a book both were able to read independently, then reading that book independently. The pair could meet before reading to explore the questions for that stage, meet at intervals during their independent reading of the book (perhaps when both had completed a chapter) to explore the questions for that stage, and meet after the whole book had been read independently to explore the questions for that stage. The role of tutor could reciprocate from stage to stage, or from book to book.

There is at present little practical experience of this latter form of Paired Thinking. Presumably it may be preferred by some students. Nevertheless, all students should have some experience of fully interactive Paired Reading and Thinking, so they can make an informed decision about what form they prefer. Of course, what they prefer may not be the same as what is best for them.

Selection, matching and contact

Recruitment considerations are as for Paired Reading (see Chapter 3). If Paired Thinking follows from Paired Reading, the cross-ability matching procedure described for peer-tutored PR in Chapter 3 applies (also see Interface with PR, p. 93).

However, if Paired Thinking follows from independent reading in same-ability pairs, draw up a ranked list of more to less able thinkers/comprehenders, based on your professional observation and judgment. Then match first with second, third with fourth, and so on. One disadvantage of same-ability tutoring is that the two weakest students in the class will be working together. This may work reasonably well as long as they are not also the most disorganized and distractible. You will need to monitor them especially closely in any case, but don't you always? If you choose to operate same-ability peer tutoring, also consider whether roles should reciprocate in the pair, and with what frequency – per book, per session, per page?

Another possibility is to mix same-ability and cross-ability matching within the same class or group. You might choose cross-ability matching with some of your weakest students as tutees (tutored by average students), and same-ability matching with some of your most able students. But this degree of complexity is perhaps best left until you have more experience.

Contact arrangements should be as for Paired Reading (see Chapter 3), subject to the considerations in the Interface with PR section (p. 93) regarding the possibility of alternating Paired Reading and Paired Thinking in consecutive sessions.

You will need to consider how many sessions per week of what length over what period is optimum, what the optimum duration of PR before moving into PT might be, and whether alternating sessions of PR and PT would work.

Organizing contact can be problematic, especially for cross-age projects and especially in high schools. You will need to consider the synchronization of tutee and tutor timetables, finding physical spaces for the pair which is reliably available, and the possibility of over-spill into personal and social education, recess, club, or other times. Will other commitments or priorities interfere? Also rehearse how the loss of 'regular curricular time' can be defended.

Producing materials

As described in Chapter 6, each pair starts with a question prompt sheet at Level 1. After this, each pair is moved onto the next Level when the monitoring project organizer feels they are ready. The levels are intended to enable you to progressively differentiate and individualize the reading and thinking activities for different pairs, adding layers of complexity and sophistication bit by bit, without making too much work for you. Thus the complexity of the questioning framework is differentiated and adapted to the functioning and ambitions of each pair.

To help see which pairs are doing what, the prompt sheets for the different levels can be copied onto different colored paper (or card), so the levels are color-coded.

Alternatively, you could copy the Before, During and After stages onto three different colors, especially for Levels 3 and 4.

All four levels are provided as electronic files, and can be downloaded from the TRW website. From these you may want to differentiate even further, producing your own Level 1A, or Level 1A and Level 1B, for instance, to help bridge between Level 1 and Level 2 for the weaker or less confident children.

You may wish to abbreviate some levels, or to adapt the materials for your students in some other way, perhaps expressing the questions in much simpler language or the local vernacular.

You may also want to use the electronic files to produce versions in larger or more compressed type, or in a different layout, to suit your children.

The Tips for Tutors Reminder Sheet is also available as an electronic file. You can produce your own shorter version of what you consider to be the most important ones if you wish, and add the less important ones cumulatively as you go along.

Once tutors have been exposed to all the tips, consult the tutors and tutees about which tips now seem the most important to them.

With experience, tutors (and maybe tutees) may be able to suggest additional questions to include in the prompt sheets. If there is consensus about the value of certain additional questions, it is easy to incorporate them in your master electronic file.

As with Paired Reading, you also need to consider access to reading material. Access to reading materials must be swift, easy and reliable. The system for access to books needs careful monitoring to ensure it is actually working. The book supply may need changing to fill any emerging gaps, to be more appropriate, or just to refresh the project.

Using materials

For the training sessions and for the immediately following regular sessions, all pairs start with a Level 1 prompt sheet. Mostly the tutor will look at this. All tutors also have the Tips for Tutors Reminder Sheet.

As pairs progress in subsequent sessions, issue pairs with Level 2, 3 and 4 prompt sheets as you judge appropriate. Level 2 is intended to be a relatively small step from Level 1 (to encourage all concerned), so all pairs should eventually progress to Level 2. However, progression to Levels 3 and 4 will be much more dependent upon the different abilities of individual pairs.

Level 4 is obviously very elaborate and over-inclusive, indeed perhaps better suited to high school or even college students.

Training

For peer tutoring with elementary school children, training should be scheduled for two separate sessions, each of half an hour, within the same week. For parent or volunteer training, or peer tutoring with older children with a longer attention span, one session of one hour is likely to be more convenient. In either event, the content and activities fall naturally into two parts (A and B). As with all paired learning methods, train tutors and tutees together.

Training Session Part A

In the first introductory training session, make clear that this is an extension to reading together, not something completely new or different.

Explain how Paired Thinking has 3 Stages, 13 Activities, lots of Questions, 4 Levels and 21 Tips for Tutors.

Give the pairs the Level 1 prompt sheets and talk them through the main points.

Then give out the Tips for Tutors Reminder document and talk both tutors and tutees through all the points. You can use the fuller Tips for Tutors document as a script if you wish. Leave the tutors with the materials to read and think about and say you will be revisiting them later.

Training Session Part B

At the second training session, spend the first ten minutes (or so) reading a short book or self-explanatory chapter to all the pairs, telling them that they will be practicing Paired Thinking on the book when you have finished. Especially with elementary school students, it is advantageous if this book is in a large format for group use.

Choice of the book is tricky: should it be fiction or non-fiction? The difficulty of the book should be aimed at the reading comprehension level of an average student (then even the weakest student has a good chance of understanding most of it on the basis of listening comprehension).

Pretend to be a tutor in relation to the book. Model asking some of the questions from the Level 1 prompt sheet, treating the whole training group as your tutees. Solicit answers from any tutor or tutee, from as many different participants as will offer answers.

Be sure you model developing a gentle and encouraging demeanor while questioning, and model the process of always responding with further questions which give clues, and/or with praise, but never with 'yes', 'no', 'that's right', 'that's wrong!'.

Obviously it is difficult to demonstrate the Before questions on a book you have just unilaterally chosen to read to the whole group, but do the best you can.

Then change roles. You play the part of a tutee, and encourage all the participants to pretend to be your tutor and to ask you some of the questions. They should have their Level 1 prompt sheets to hand to help them.

It is important you also model a 'think-aloud', so tutors and tutees understand what is meant by this. If you have colleagues present, they can act as stooge tutees in the audience and fill in any gaps in the conversation.

Tell the pairs they will start doing Paired Thinking for themselves on whatever book they choose at their next session together.

Compared to Paired Reading, Paired Thinking will obviously involve more discussion and the pair will not progress through the book as fast as they might expect or wish. Reassure them that this is what you expect and encourage, provided they are actually talking about something relevant to their reading. They 'need to take more time so they can think better'.

Also, prepare them from the outset for some brain strain – Paired Thinking is considerably more challenging than Paired Reading, especially for the tutor, and especially for younger, less able and near-age tutors. Some pairs will not like their comfort zone being stretched. Reassure them that Paired Thinking is very good for them (tutors and tutees), even if it might not always feel it at the time. Try marketing PT to students as a maturational progression from PR, a more grown-up thing to do.

Put great emphasis on the tutor's active listening and striving to support and develop (or scaffold) the tutee's response by asking further detailed questions or giving clues or prompts, but never just giving what the tutor thinks is the 'right' answer. Acknowledge that this is not easy, and will make the tutor think hard as well. However, take care not to give the impression that the tutor interrogates the tutee. Tutees should soon come to feel sufficiently supported and

relaxed that they are able to 'think aloud' without any fear of immediately eliciting another tiresome question.

Most of the questions (in all Levels) are about what the tutee
thinks. You may feel that questions about feelings (emotional
responses to the book) are too few. You can easily insert more in your
master electronic file. Or, if you find that this is difficult because
feeling questions tend to relate closely to the content of the particular book, issue general encouragement to pairs about this in training
and monitoring.

If you feel this is too much for your children to absorb in the
training format outlined above, think about introducing the 'stages'
on different days in sequence – cover 'Before Reading' first, then
'During Reading' another day a little later, then 'After Reading' a
day or two later still.

The minimal training will almost certainly be too brief to generate high quality practice in all pairs. Further training and/or coaching is likely to be needed, especially with younger, less able and near-
age tutors, and especially with non-fiction books. Issues that should
be addressed in more detailed onward training include:

- What exactly might all the prompt questions mean?
- When do you fit in the questions without breaking the
  flow?
- How exactly do you 'prompt by asking another question'?
- How does the tutor judge if a question is too difficult for the
  tutee?

The students will certainly offer some interesting suggestions in
response to these questions, and some of them might be practical.

Monitoring and support

Regular, frequent and reliable monitoring is essential, and planning
must ensure that this can be easily and consistently delivered and
sustained. This will involve the reliable release of staff for this purpose (as for training).

When monitoring peer-tutored Paired Thinking sessions, the
project organizer's first task is always to check which tutors and

tutees are absent. Members of incomplete pairs can be re-matched, and you may have standby tutors as in Paired Reading. However, you will need to think about how re-matching might work if the original tutor is away from school and you have a supply tutor – who will be completely reliant on the tutee's interpretation of the book because the tutor probably will not have read it.

Close monitoring of what the children are actually doing in their pairs is crucial to the success of this approach. In a peer tutoring project, the project organizer must circulate to see how the pairs are coping. If a parent and child are doing Paired Thinking at home, it is just as important that the parent and child have access to support, monitoring and trouble-shooting from school or other appropriate source. You may wish to design a Paired Thinking Home-School Diary based on the PR Diary (see TRW website).

Any extra help you can obtain with monitoring and further coaching will prove invaluable, especially for the early sessions when tutors and tutees are finding their way and are least practiced and least confident.

A Paired Thinking Technique Checklist is provided (on the TRW website) for you to copy and use to structure and (if you wish) record your observations of pairs. Do not always target the pairs you see (or expect) to be having difficulty. You also need to visit other pairs at random. Do not assume that all is well just because it seems to be going smoothly on the surface.

Make sure each pair has the appropriate level prompt sheet and the tutor is referring to it. Make sure the tutor is referring to the Tips Reminder sheet. Point out to each pair what they are doing well and what they need to do better (the Tips are numbered to help with this). If necessary, model the behavior required for the tutor with the tutee. Watch carefully for the quality of active listening and scaffolding by the tutors (asking further detailed questions or giving clues or prompts) but never just giving what the tutor thinks is the 'right' answer.

Remember Paired Thinking will be especially difficult for your least able tutors. Also, you will need to think about how the least able pairs can do Paired Thinking with a book which may only have a word or two on each page.

Even for able tutors, PT involves considerable brain strain, so be sure to regularly reassure tutors that this is normal and to be expected, and is a result of graduating to a more adult way of doing things. Give tutors a great deal of praise and appreciation to make them feel the effort is worth it. It is likely to be some time before they see the benefits for themselves.

The During activities are the most complex and demanding, and most at risk of not being done well. Take especial care to support the quality of During activity with your pairs. Watch out for pairs mechanically chanting through the given prompt questions, perhaps even in the given order, and intervene. They should be thinking up their own questions, responding strategically to the specific issues of the book they are reading. Do not get drawn into debates about content and giving the 'right answer'. Your mission is to help them ask intelligent questions.

Reassure pairs that 'taking more time so they can think better' is OK, and indeed encouraged provided they are actually talking about something relevant to their reading. Deal with the frustration a child with rigid expectations may be feeling.

In peer tutoring, give all pairs a reminder five minutes before the session is due to end, so they can get some thinking in at the end of the session if they have forgotten to do any during the earlier part of the session. But obviously encourage discussion during the whole session as well.

Your observations while monitoring will indicate when each pair is ready to move on to the next level.

Once pairs are in the swing of it, you may want to make an audio or video recording of one or two particularly competent pairs at work. This can be very valuable as a demonstration in subsequent training meetings, as well as interesting in its own right and a valuable tool for self-assessment by the pair. Once you have some children who are competent in the method, consider a demonstration role play with a particularly competent and confident child or pair at a training session. But you would still need to demonstrate Paired Thinking on a story or book with which all pairs were already familiar.

Evaluation

The evaluation of Paired Thinking projects is considered in detail in

Chapter 9. An especially critical question is how generalization to reading and thinking across the curriculum can be promoted and ensured, and how this can be measured.

8 Does Paired Thinking Work?

Co-authors:
Whitney Barrett, Angela Bryce and Janie McKinstery

Paired Thinking is a relatively new development and the research on its effectiveness consequently modest in volume. While it contains elements that have proved effective in other related programs, this particular combination of elements delivered in this particular way obviously needs detailed evaluation in its own right.

Some research has been completed in peer-tutored Paired Thinking, and more is in progress. Evaluation of the extension of the method to parents and children at home, and to volunteers, is needed. Any readers who are conducting related research are encouraged to contact the author.

Evaluating improvements in quality of thinking is not a straightforward task, however, as Chapter 9 explicates. Much of the evaluation of Paired Reading to date has focussed on measuring improvements in reading comprehension, rather than more generalized improvements in quality of thinking.

Paired Thinking was first introduced to thirteen elementary schools in Scotland. In all cases this was on a cross-age, cross-ability peer tutoring basis, and followed eight to ten weeks of Paired Reading. This was the Read On pilot project (Chapter 4 reports the outcomes from the Paired Reading phase of this project). Subsequently many other schools adopted the approach, but did not build in formal evaluation.

A more intensive study of a peer-tutored Paired Thinking project in one elementary school in Scotland was then conducted, incorporating focussed assessment of changes in thinking skills rather than broad-spectrum reading comprehension skills (the Bryce Project). The peer-tutored method was then piloted in a high school (the McKinstery project).

Read On: reading test results

Not all the pilot schools felt able to mount the extension from Paired Reading to Paired Thinking, although the majority did. However, in those schools implementing Paired Thinking, practice was varied. A few schools had three sessions of Paired Thinking per week, some only one, which was unlikely to yield a measurable difference in student performance. Additionally, some schools ended their Paired Thinking after a brief trial, while others continued for longer periods. Measures of implementation integrity were not available for the Paired Thinking phase (although they were for the Paired Reading phase).

The norm-referenced group test of reading comprehension used as an outcome measure was expected to show an increase, and some correlation with increased thinking skills was assumed. However, Paired Thinking actually involved less time reading and more time discussing than Paired Reading, so a paradoxical effect was possible. In short, it is far from clear what the reading test results were actually measuring. These difficulties were further compounded when only nine of the thirteen schools were able to complete the follow-up test before the end of the academic year.

A further complication is that reading test norms typically track the progress of children over a full calendar year, while the school year is shorter, and progress over the school year may be uneven. For instance, it is possible that most of the growth in reading ability occurs in the autumn and spring, as the weeks in school before the summer vacation are often devoted to wider ranging activities, and little reading may be done by children during the long summer vacation itself. If this is the case, to sustain a normal rate of growth in reading during the weeks in school before the summer vacation might be construed as a good outcome.

Indeed, the results for control group students upheld this hypothesis: 70 per cent showed a fall in standardized scores from post-test levels. This suggests that to have showed no change in reading growth at this time of the school year is indeed a good outcome.

Of those schools which implemented Paired Thinking, for tutees seven classes showed no increase, three showed an increase which did not reach statistical significance, and one showed an increase which did reach statistical significance. For tutors five classes showed no increase, four showed increases which did not reach statistical significance, and one showed increases which did reach statistical significance (it was not possible to collect data for the other tutor classes). Many of the groups were small, so that finding statistical significance was inherently unlikely. These data suggest that tutors benefited most consistently from Paired Thinking in terms of the crude measure of reading comprehension used.

However, there is a further difficulty of interpretation. As noted in Chapter 4, Paired Reading by itself has been found to produce continuing reading growth after the intensive period of involvement. Although this finding is based more on studies of parent tutoring than of peer tutoring, it is possible that the continuing advantage of experimental over control students was due to the enduring effect of Paired Reading, rather than any additive effect of Paired Thinking.

Read On: student feedback

At one of the pilot project schools, qualitative exploration of the feelings of the participant Paired Thinking tutors and tutees was undertaken (Barrett, 1999). This was done in two consecutive Circle Time sessions, held early and later in the Paired Thinking experience. Tutees and tutors had separate sessions.

At the first session, the children split into pairs to discuss how Paired Thinking was different from Paired Reading. The facilitator emphasized that there were no right or wrong answers. When the whole group reconvened, each child was invited to share some of the things they had been discussing. After this, each child was asked to offer a single word to describe Paired Thinking.

The second session followed the same pattern: pairs discussed which they liked best, Paired Reading or Paired Thinking, and why they chose the answer they did. The facilitator emphasized that there were no right or wrong answers. When the whole group reconvened, each child was invited to share some of the things they had been discussing. After this, each child was asked to offer a single word to describe Paired Thinking.

Only some of the more interesting insights from the participants are reported here (full details are available on the Read On website).

While the tutors were aged 10, the tutees were only 7, and this is reflected in the nature of the comments.

Tutee first session
Paired Thinking is different from Paired Reading because:

- you get new questions and more questions
- you get new partners
- you get to ask your partner questions
- you get prompt cards
- you get 21 top tips.

Paired Thinking is:

good, brilliant, excellent, brilliant, extra-good, fantabulous, extra-fantastic, good, superb, triple good, extra-fabulous, hard.

(This looks as if the class teacher had been working on the vocabulary of praise.)

Tutee second session
I like Paired Reading best because:

- you don't get questions (girl)
- you don't get as much questions (boy)
- you don't get to answer questions (boy)
- you get less questions (boy).
- I liked the partner I had for Paired Reading (boy)

I like Paired Thinking best because:

- you get new books and a new partner (girl)
- you get more questions (girl)
- you get new partners (girl)
- you get prompt cards and sheets for your tutor to fill in. You also get a bigger range of books (girl)
- you get prompt cards and a change of partner (girl)
- you get harder books and get asked more questions (girl)
- you get a new partner, prompt sheets and more questions and sometimes you can laugh at the questions (girl)

- I got the partner I wanted (boy).

(There does seem to be some evidence of a sex bias in post-experience attitudes to Paired Thinking here.)

Paired Thinking is:
good, excellent, brilliant, fantastic, fabulous, excellent, good, great, fabulous, excellent, brilliant, fabulous, brilliant.

Tutor first session
Paired Thinking is different from Paired Reading because:
Answers included: that Paired Thinking involves more questioning than Paired Reading, there are prompt cards and other new materials such as Tips for Tutors and a revised diary, and that pairs do not do as much actual reading in Paired Thinking as they do during Paired Reading. Problems included the difficulty some tutors and tutees had understanding some of the prompt questions and that not all of these were appropriate for the book being read.

Paired Thinking is:
Most acknowledged that Paired Thinking was more difficult than Paired Reading for both the tutees and the tutors. Some tutors thought this was an advantage because it 'stretched' all those involved more, while others thought this was a distinct disadvantage.

Tutor second session
I like Paired Reading best because:

- there's not so many questions (girl)
- there's some questions, but not so many as Paired Thinking (girl)
- Paired Thinking has too many questions and sometimes the tutors don't understand the questions themselves (girl)
- there's not as much questions (boy)
- my tutee now (for Paired Thinking) is too bossy (girl)
- the Paired Thinking questions are a bit hard for the younger ones and sometimes I don't understand the questions (boy)
- when you do Paired Thinking you have to interrupt the

book you're reading, but you don't have to with Paired Reading (boy)

- with Paired Thinking you don't get as far with the book. You can't get onto the next chapter (boy)
- when you've got a good book you don't like asking questions, because you won't get it finished (girl)
- because it's much easier for everyone (boy)
- because it's helpful (girl)
- because there's not as much questions to ask the younger ones (girl)
- because you can chat to the child and it's more socializing (girl).

I like Paired Thinking best because:

- the children don't just pick up any book they think will be easy, because you've got a sheet with questions on that you must ask them (girl)
- you get a different tutee and you get harder books (girl)
- it encourages both the tutor and the tutee to read more (boy)
- it will be better for us when we go to high school and it's better for the little ones too (boy).

Paired Thinking is:

hard, sociable, okay, wonderful, easy, more harder, superb, okay, difficult, hard, all right, difficult, brilliant, excellent, tempting, educational, a wee bit harder although sometimes it's OK.

These qualitative responses give a rich picture and a similar picture has emerged in other projects. Overall, it seems that Paired Thinking was popular with tutees, but less popular than Paired Reading with some of the tutors, for whom it involved a lot of strenuous thinking. However, the test gains reported above were highest for the tutors. It seems the correlation between gain and pain was not apparent to everyone.

The Bryce Project

This project sought better quality evidence of improvement in thinking skills from cross-age peer tutoring in Paired Thinking. It also aimed to explore the added value for thinking skills of moving from Paired Reading into Paired Thinking, as compared to continuing with Paired Reading (Topping and Bryce, submitted).

In one elementary school, two classes of eleven-year-old students were tutors, matched with tutees from two classes of seven-year-olds. Class size ranged from 27 to 31. The two experimental classes and the two comparison classes engaged in a six-week Paired Reading program. After a three-week school vacation, the experimental class engaged in Paired Thinking for ten weeks, while the comparison class continued with Paired Reading for the same period.

The time allocated and the interactive nature of the activity during that time was the same for both experimental and comparison groups. The thinking skills and attitude towards reading of tutors and tutees in both the PT and PR groups were assessed before and after the program. Implementation integrity of the program was carefully monitored, and additional qualitative measures were used to triangulate assessment of development in thinking skills.

Thinking skills programs such as Instrumental Enrichment (IE) continue for two years, and in the case of IE evidence for short-term gains is equivocal (see Chapter 6). The PT program in this research operated for one session of twenty minutes per week for ten weeks, after a 30-minute training for tutors and tutees. It was therefore considered that the likelihood of finding measurable gains in thinking skills was not high, especially as the comparison was with a group receiving an alternative treatment already known to be highly effective, rather than with a non-participant control group.

The host school was an elementary school with approximately 300 students, situated in a city in Scotland, in an area of above average socio-economic status. The school had previous experience with PR, and reading standards were generally already high. In the first phase, Paired Reading was programed for all groups for twenty minutes per week for six weeks. In the second phase, the same frequency of sessions continued for a further ten weeks, either in PT or PR format. All sessions occurred on the same day and at the same time for all students. The pairs also operated alternately in the tutors' and the tutees' classroom, and so were equally exposed to each teacher. After the initial PR phase, all students in all groups received a pre-test on thinking skills prior to Phase 2.

Eighty books (40 fiction and 40 non-fiction) were selected by the researcher and divided into four boxes to provide a balanced selection of reading material for each class. These boxes were rotated every three weeks. By the end of the program all students had had access to the same core supply of books. This was a very small resource, and the tutees could also choose to read a book selected on their weekly visit to the library.

One older class and one younger class were considered more able than the parallel classes and were therefore matched together. A group reading test was given to all students and pairs then matched on the basis of the results as described in Chapter 7. No adjustments due to social factors were made. High ability spare tutors initially acted as standby tutors and peer monitors.

Assignment of classes to conditions was not done until the end of the all-PR Phase 1. This was done on purpose. One class teacher was expected to leave, and this class and its parallel were allocated to the continuing PR condition as being less disruptive for the children. In the event, this plan later went astray, and the teacher from the experimental PT tutor class left.

The teachers further differentiated the four levels of question prompt sheet, and color-coded the levels. A new starting level below Level 1 was created as well as other intermediate levels. In order to bridge the skills being learned in the program to other curriculum activities, the experimental teachers agreed to model the questions when hearing individual children's reading and to use the framework during normal classroom discussion of texts. The PT tutors' teacher would also spend some time before each session reminding tutors of the process and going over the new questions with those moving onto a higher level.

PT training took place in the dining hall with both tutors and tutees of the experimental group and their teachers present. The trainer brought large format fiction and non-fiction books, which could be easily seen. Large flash cards showing individual questions were also used. Two kinds of large format book were used to demonstrate that some questions were only relevant to certain types of books. A video demonstration of PT was shown. However, time was not available for the recommended reciprocation of teacher and student role in training (see Chapter 7).

A group test to assess thinking skills during and after reading was developed, following the guidelines for an open-ended test on critical thinking proposed by Norris and Ennis (1989). Ten questions demanding a different aspect of thinking about a short story were developed. The story was taken from Fisher's (1996) *Stories for Thinking*, a collection of multi-cultural stories for children of seven–eleven years, designed to stimulate thinking. The questions were selected from the During and After Level 3 Paired Thinking framework, to avoid any ceiling effect that might occur at post-test. Since the story was from a book of short stories, offering little advance information or organizers, it was inappropriate to ask the Before Reading questions.

A table of specifications was drawn up in line with the recommendations of Norris and Ennis (1989) showing the key aspects of thinking that should be tested using the Paired Thinking questions from Level 3.

Aspects of thinking in reading

- thinking about the context
- thinking about the author's purpose
- thinking about the relationship between characters
- thinking about a character's reaction to a situation
- speculating
- inferring
- predicting
- generalizing
- summarizing
- evaluating

Owing to time constraints, it was not possible to pilot this test of thinking skills. Therefore no indication of its construct validity or reliability can be given although, as with many curriculum-based measures, face validity appears high.

Testing a class at a time, pupils were issued with the text of the short story and an answer grid containing the questions. Giving the questions before the reading may have helped the pupils' understanding of the story. The story was read aloud to the whole class, pausing at pre-determined places to ask questions and allow the children to record their answers on the answer grid.

Many of the younger children found some of the questions difficult to understand and several requested help. Encouragement was
given to try hard but they were instructed to write 'I don't know' to
any questions they did not understand. This procedure for testing
thinking skills was repeated at post-test. However, two stories of
the same level could not be identified. The post-test was more difficult and required more inference.

The tutors from the experimental group had experienced a
change of teacher towards the end of the program. At the time of
post-testing they were still adapting to this. Their behavior during,
and attitude towards, the post-test was very different from the pre-
test. They were very unsettled and on several occasions had to be
reminded not to talk and to concentrate.

Assessment of the answers to the thinking skills test was informed
by the guidelines proposed by Norris and Ennis (1989):

- Develop criteria for a good response, based upon the aspects
  of critical thinking you wish to assess, and suitable for the
  grade level being tested, but leave room for flexibility.
- When grading a student's response, first read the whole
  short answer without assigning a grade, in order to get an
  overview or sense of the student's response. Then re-read it,
  applying the criteria you have developed.
- Do not allow such things as legibility, grammar and spelling
  to influence unnecessarily your judgment of students' critical thinking. Remember what you are testing.
- If students' responses differ from the ideal response, try to
  discern why. Do not mark responses merely right or wrong
  as in multiple-choice tests, and be open to legitimate alternative responses to the outline.

When developing an outline of a good response, the four criteria
proposed by Norris and Ennis (1989) for judging explanatory inferences were used:

- the inference should explain what it is supposed to explain
- the inference should take account of all relevant textual
  information

- the inference should be consistent with background knowledge the student can reasonably be expected to have
- the inference should be better than plausible alternatives.

Criteria for each answer were developed and the pupils' responses graded on a scale of 0 to 3. A second rater, who was an experienced teacher, then independently assigned a grade to each answer for every student. Inter-rater agreement for each question for pre-test and post-test separately ranged from 96 per cent to 100 per cent, averaging 98.25 per cent.

However, there were doubts concerning the validity of this testing procedure. Firstly, the children were tested in a non-interactive situation. There is the possibility that this type of assessment did not tap into the true effects of the program, which was highly interactive and mediated. Secondly, a major barrier to some of the children demonstrating their ability in the test of thinking skills was the fact that they were required to write their answers. An individual and interactive test in which items were presented orally might be expected to be more sensitive to experimental effects, although much more time consuming.

The Elementary Reading Attitude Survey (ERAS) (McKenna and Kear, 1990) was used pre- and post-test to measure the pupils' attitudes towards reading. It was administered on a group basis to a class at a time according to the procedure in the manual, except that the researcher read each question aloud, giving the children time to record their answers.

Weekly visits to the school ensured that both the PR and PT programs were implemented correctly. The teachers involved directly observed some pairs during each session, recording their observations on the PT Technique Checklist (see TRW website). During the third week of Phase 2, the standby tutors appeared somewhat underemployed, and were formed into a subgroup for same-age reciprocal Paired Thinking at Level 3. Outcomes for this small subgroup were not evaluated.

From the ranked listings based on the group reading tests, every fourth boy and every fourth girl were selected to join a feedback discussion group at the end of the program. The tutor and tutee discussion groups met separately. The children were very forthcoming in expressing their opinions.

The quantitative data were assumed to meet many of the requirements for using parametric statistical tests, although sampling was
not random. Independent and paired samples t-tests were therefore
used to assess statistical significance. There was no significant difference in scores of thinking skills from pre-test to post-test for either
the PR or PT tutor groups, although the PT group started somewhat
higher than the PR group. There was a great deal more variance in
scores in the experimental tutors at post-test.

For tutees, at pre-test there was no difference in thinking skills
between the PR and PT groups. At post-test, the PT tutees' scores were
significantly higher than those of the comparison tutees ($t = 3.22$, df
46, $p < 0.01$). The PT group sustained the same level of performance on
the harder test, but the comparison group scores fell.

There was no significant difference in attitude to recreational
reading between the experimental and comparison tutors before or
after the intervention.

There was no significant difference in attitude to recreational
reading between the experimental and comparison tutees before
the intervention. However, at post-test the experimental tutees'
mean score in attitude to recreational reading was significantly
higher than that of the comparison tutees ($t = 3.22$, df 46, $p < 0.01$).
A similar result was found for academic reading ($t = 2.70$, df 51,
$p < 0.5$).

Comments made by the experimental tutors and tutees during the
feedback sessions are recorded below (repetitions and irrelevancies
are not given).

Tutees

'You did Paired Reading for a while and then you did Paired Reading
and Thinking. What did you think about Paired Reading and Thinking?'

- I preferred Paired Reading, because some questions were
  hard.
- I preferred Paired Thinking, because my partner asked me
  questions.
- I liked hard questions.
- The questions were harder with nonfiction books.

- It was much harder with fact books.
- I liked the question about my favorite part.
- I didn't understand some questions, like 'What does the author want?'
- The questions slowed you down, and you don't have so much time to read the books.
- There were too many questions.
- It would have been better with some new books.

Tutors

'You did Paired Reading for a while and then you did Paired Reading and Thinking. What did you think about Paired Reading and Thinking?'

- It was hard to fit in the questions.
- There were too many questions.
- It would have been better to have involved the tutees in making up three questions during the training session, and then you could be sure that they would understand them.
- I didn't know where to stop to ask the questions.
- My tutee kept turning the page and I couldn't fit the questions in.
- It was annoying having to stop all the time to ask questions.
- My tutee sometimes asked me a hard question and I didn't know the answer.
- Some of the questions were too difficult for my tutee.
- The poetry books were really difficult to ask questions about.
- I think my tutee started choosing a better variety of books during Paired Thinking.
- I preferred Paired Reading because you got through more books.

Findings from the discussion sessions indicate that most of the children in the experimental group seemed to enjoy the social aspect of the project, apart from those pairings which had not worked particularly well. In general, the tutees seemed more positive about Paired Reading and Thinking, with a few reporting that they enjoyed the questions. Negative comments about the difficulty of the questions (especially with non-fiction books) and the interruption to reading that they caused were common to both tutors and tutees.

There was general agreement among the teachers of the experimental groups that asking open-ended questions was the most difficult activity for the tutors. One teacher also thought that the children found it difficult to find appropriate breaks to ask questions, especially when they did not know the text. The tutors had however appeared to find it easy to make up their own questions, prompt the tutee and give time to answer. The teacher of the experimental tutors (who was with them for most of the program but left three weeks before the end of the intervention) considered that, in general, the thinking skills of the tutors had improved. Thus her observations did not concur with the thinking test results for the tutors. Both teachers of the experimental group reported that they would use the program again.

However, knowing about effective thinking is not enough. Students have to want to use that knowledge. Perhaps for the experimental tutors, the failure to show a significant gain in thinking skills was due to a lack of enthusiasm for PT, or a lack of enthusiasm for the test situation which mirrored the actual program. Perhaps the tutors did not feel inclined to use the thinking skills in the test situation that the teacher felt they had developed.

There was also a decline at post-test in the experimental tutors' attitudes to academic reading. Poor post-test performance in these two quite disparate tests suggests a general disinclination on the part of the experimental tutors to be bothered with tests. The researcher had observed a general restlessness and lack of effort and concentration in the PT tutor class during the post-testing. This may have been due to their recent change of teacher, and consequent adaptation to a different style of teaching and classroom management.

The experimental tutors' lack of effort at post-test may also have been due to their limited enthusiasm for Paired Thinking. Comments made by the tutors showed a less positive attitude to PT than tutees. This supports findings from previous evaluations of Paired Thinking, where the tutors expressed a preference for Paired Reading. Tutors found Paired Thinking hard work. Stopping to ask questions interrupted their enjoyment of the book.

Paired Thinking requires a great many skills from the tutors. They need to promote a positive relationship by listening, supporting, encouraging and praising. They are required to scaffold the tutees' learning by making explicit the meta-cognitive processes involved in reading. They have to judge what questions to ask and when to ask them, to explain or give answers when necessary, and to give appropriate thinking time to the tutee.

The high expectation that children would be able to operationalize these various strategies was mentioned by one of the teachers in this study. Discussing how difficult it was for the tutors to find an appropriate break to ask questions, she considered that, without knowing the text, this was a very demanding task. 'This is a high expectation for children of this age. It is a skill we develop as teachers and it is a lot to ask of the children.'

In this study the tutors themselves commented on the difficulty of fitting in the questions, and expressed their reservations about asking the tutees questions which were too difficult. This seems to reflect the difficulty they had adjusting the level of difficulty of the questions to allow them to work in the tutees' zone of proximal development (the zone between level of difficulty at which the tutee can perform unaided and the higher level at which they can perform with support, but not at so high a level that they do not succeed even with support).

More intensive training for tutors before and during the training should be considered in future studies of Paired Reading and Thinking. More emphasis on praise for tutors seems indicated, since they clearly feel the cognitive stress of the Paired Thinking task and should have their efforts fully acknowledged and appreciated. Modeling and monitoring from supervising teachers should also focus on these issues.

In this study, the core supply of books was modest. A change or re-supply of books might have renewed the children's motivation for the program as they entered the PT component. The comments of the children regarding the relative difficulty of PT with non-fiction books is another issue to bear in mind.

Perhaps future research could explore the effects of planned reciprocation in same-ability pairs within a Paired Reading context, where a more symmetrical relationship may encourage both tutor and tutee to give explanations to promote their cognitive development.

It was unlikely that this program, which ran for one twenty-minute session once a week for ten weeks, would result in any significant difference in thinking skills. The fact that it did for the tutees must be highlighted as a finding of considerable importance, with strong implications for cost-effectiveness.

Adey and Shayer (1994) suggest that some immediate post-tests underestimate the effects of intervention – there may be 'sleeper effects'. Follow-up assessment of the tutees prior to transfer to high school would seem worthwhile.

The McKinstery project

This Paired Thinking project in a high school was organizationally interesting in many ways. It was led, coordinated and monitored internally by the head of the mathematics department, although the English department was also involved. The high school was a non-denominational co-educational school of 1200 students, serving four small urban areas surrounded by rural communities, near the west coast of Scotland. Students lived within a ten-mile radius in an area with a mixture of subsidized and private housing. The school had no previous history of implementation of Paired Reading.

The tutors were volunteers from the fifth and sixth year (sixteen- to eighteen-year-olds). Eighteen initially volunteered (fourteen girls and six boys). One withdrew after the first training meeting, and a further two dropped out subsequently, leaving fifteen. Initially seventeen tutees were randomly chosen from one mixed-ability class group in first year (twelve-year-olds). The intention was to evaluate the program with a broad-spectrum population and avoid any stigmatization as a special needs initiative. (For further details see McKinstery and Topping, submitted.)

The large age and ability gap between tutors and tutees meant that resulting reading gains for the tutors were unlikely, although gains in thinking and social skills might be possible. This cross-age format reflected the preference of the school, not that of the external consultant-researchers. It was not possible to establish control groups. However, the relatively high levels of ability, maturity and insight in the tutor group meant that their own reflective observations on their experiences were likely to be a rich source of information.

It was agreed that there should be free student selection of reading materials from the school library and the English department collection, both fiction and non-fiction. Training meetings were first held for the tutors only, then for the tutors and tutees together. Owing to organizational constraints, the PR training took place just before the Christmas vacation, while tutoring activity started after the vacation. Only one person was available for monitoring PR practice during this session.

Paired Reading operated for four weeks, then further training meetings preceded the move to Paired Thinking, which operated for a further five weeks. At the first PT meeting for tutors, emphasis was placed upon the fact that the question prompt sheets were merely basic scripts, which should be adapted and elaborated depending on the reading material and the interaction between tutor and tutee. At the second training meeting with both tutors and tutees, the reading exemplar used was Roald Dahl's *The Witches*, selected to be engaging across the wide age gap between tutors and tutees.

PR and PT sessions took place three times per week. Each session lasted approximately twenty minutes. Owing to the differing time-tables of the tutors, session days and times were idiosyncratic to each pair, and required complex synchronization from the coordinating teacher. Tutees had to be released from several subject classes throughout the week. The tutors and tutees were largely responsible for ensuring their own meetings actually took place. In order to allow the pairings to be accommodated in quiet areas, the school library and the senior social area were made available for the sessions. The pairs decided where they would meet. A researcher monitored the sessions weekly, but given the idiosyncratic meeting times, could visit only a few pairs each time. Interim meetings were also held with the tutors to review and check technique.

Objective evaluation comprised a brief group norm-referenced reading comprehension test on a pre–post basis for the tutees only. The tutors were too able in reading to be effectively tested, and unlikely to make reading test gains. As the pre-test was conducted before the start of the combined PR + PT program, and post-test at the end, it is not possible to partial the effects of the two program components on test performance.

Fifteen tutees were tested, with a mean chronological age of 12 years 5 months. Reading ages (grade level equivalent) were calculated from their test performance. At pre-test the mean reading age was 13 years 2 months. At post-test the mean reading age was 14 years 0 months. This represents an increase in reading age of ten months over a four-month intervention period. This gain is much greater than would be expected over a normal four-month period, and was statistically significant (Wilcoxon $Z = 2.093$, $p < 0.05$, 2-tailed).

	n	Minimum	Maximum	Mean	Standard Deviation
Pre-test	15	108.00	183.00	158.466	25.0709
Post-test	15	129.00	183.00	168.400	17.6708

A simple written measure of attitude to reading was completed on a pre–post basis by the tutees, but no significant changes were evident. A simple written measure of self-concept was also completed on a pre–post basis by the tutees, but no significant changes were evident.

Considering the responses of the tutees to a subjective feedback questionnaire (see TRW website), 70 per cent thought the Paired Thinking had been as they expected it to be pre-implementation. Of those who did not, the main reason given was the difficulty in making arrangements to meet their tutor. However, only 48 per cent of tutees said that they liked Paired Thinking, although 66 per cent stated that they had been happy with their tutor.

Tutee statements concerning what they liked about Paired Thinking included:

- The discussions were enjoyable (more than half the tutees said this)
- The tutor was friendly
- The tutor explained the book/words
- Getting out of regular classes
- Paired Thinking was hard.

When asked what they disliked about Paired Thinking:

- 33 per cent stated that they disliked the questioning as they found it difficult
- 13.3 per cent found the tutee/tutor relationship problematic
- 20 per cent found that meeting their tutor could be difficult
- 10 per cent found that subject teachers could be unwilling to release them from classes.

However, when asked if they found it easy to answer questions during the session, 70 per cent of tutees answered in the affirmative.

Tutors also completed a subjective feedback questionnaire on their Paired Thinking experiences (see TRW website). Sixty per cent of tutors stated that they asked questions throughout the sessions, while 40 per cent asked questions only at the start or end of a session. When asked to estimate how many questions they asked per session, 60 per cent of tutors estimated that they asked five or more, the remainder estimating three or less. This rather low level of self-reported compliance to program expectations suggests that these pairs spent more time in PR mode than PT mode.

However, tutors considered 50 per cent of the questions asked were predictive, 30 per cent searching for meaning and 20 per cent evaluative. Thus, although there might have been some tendency to ask relatively few questions, and in some cases to minimize questioning during reading, it may be that the quality of questioning was cognitively of a high order. This would be unsurprising given the high ability and high motivation of these volunteer tutors.

Asked if they had utilized the prompt sheet during sessions, none of the tutors said that they had. The majority (80 per cent) stated that they had read the prompt sheet prior to sessions to use as a guideline for their own version of questioning. Eighty per cent of tutors also stated that they had moved up the levels of questioning, starting at Level 2 and moving to Level 3 or 4.

Seventy per cent of tutors reported that the tutee had also asked questions. When asked if they had been able to find answers and had developed good reasons for these answers, 70 per cent of the tutors responded in the affirmative. The remainder said that this aspect of the process had stretched their thinking skills.

When asked to estimate the main topics of discussion during a session, 90 per cent of tutors stated that the discussion focussed on the reading material, with predicting, searching for meaning, summarizing and evaluating being the foci of discussions. When asked if the discussions were productive, 70 per cent of tutors stated that they were. All tutors stated that they and their tutees had listened to one another, and avoided dominating the discourse.

Tutors were asked about progression in or transference of thinking skills. Ninety per cent thought that their own thinking skills and those of their tutee had improved. Supporting statements included:

- The tutee became more adept at reasoning
- Discussing things that the tutee did not understand helped me to elaborate on my thinking
- I had to respond to the tutee's questions which helped me to analyse more.

The group of tutors were engaged in a written reflective SWOT (Strengths, Weaknesses, Opportunities, Threats) analysis before and after the program. The pre-program SWOT revealed their positive and negative expectations (including anxieties), while the post-program SWOT enabled them to relate those expectations to the reality of their tutoring experiences.

Tutors reporting that their expectations of PT had been fulfilled included:

- improved tutor communication skills
- aided the development of the tutee's reading skills
- aided the development of the tutor's reading skills.

Their expectation that the technique and process was difficult and rigid had not been fulfilled. Also not fulfilled was the expectation of a difficult relationship with the tutee.

When asked if they had managed three sessions of Paired Thinking per week, only 40 per cent of the tutors responded in the affirmative, 20 per cent stating that they met on a fairly regular basis, and 40 per cent only managing one or two sessions on a regular basis. Reasons given for this were:

- other commitments in school
- exam revision/study time – 40 per cent
- tutor/tutee absences – 30 per cent
- illness – one tutor.

Seventy per cent of tutors described their relationship with their tutee as very good or excellent, while the remainder described it as good.

On the subject of meeting for sessions, 20 per cent of tutors made arrangements to meet at a specific location in the school, while 80 per cent of tutors collected tutees from their class. Two reasons were given for going to tutees' classes. The main reason was to avoid the possibility of class teachers not releasing tutees. The other reason was to maximize the possibility of finding one another, as the prearranged location was not always free.

Tutors were asked if their tutee was cooperative and motivated. Ninety per cent felt that their tutee was both cooperative and very motivated. The only highlighted difficulty was that some tutees did not arrive with reading material on a regular basis and some of the session had to be given up to finding a book.

Tutors were asked how being involved in the project had made them feel. Eighty per cent stated that it had made them feel good. The main reasons given were:

- helping the tutee to improve their skills and confidence
- it improved the tutor's reading/thinking ability/communication and social skills
- it made tutors feel more confident about relationships with younger students
- it gave a sense of responsibility
- Paired Thinking developed skills for those interested in teaching
- it prepares you for having children as it helps you to understand children.

Tutors were asked to suggest any changes they would make to the implementation. Suggested changes were:

- longer sessions/fewer times per week
- specific/permanent arrangements for accommodation
- timed not to coincide with exam revision/study.

SWOT analyses were also conducted pre- and post-program with the two members of school staff most involved with the program (the coordinating principal teacher of mathematics and the English teacher of the tutees). The post-intervention SWOT revealed that staff perceptions of strengths and opportunities were:

- tutee reading skills and confidence were increased
- participation was not restricted to tutees with reading difficulties
- encouraged responsibility for both tutors and tutees
- tutees became more critically aware in reading owing to PT
- tutors gained in communication and cooperative working skills
- tutor could add the program to their curriculum vitae
- the program could be further developed in the school in future school sessions
- other teachers and departments within the school could become involved
- the program was an excellent opportunity to give recognition and praise to students.

Staff perceptions of weaknesses were:

- some tutors dropped out during the implementation
- tutors lost study time
- timetabling and release of tutees from classes could be problematic.

Staff perceptions of possible threats were:

- lack of tutor commitment
- lack of tutee commitment
- lack of support from teachers not directly involved in the implementation
- lack of parental support.

The perceptions emerging from the SWOT analysis were confirmed in semi-structured interviews with the staff. The staff thought that there had been an improvement in reading and thinking skills as well as confidence in all students involved. The staff thought that there were several advantages for tutors. An increased sense of responsibility was encouraged and created, owing to the onus on the tutors to ensure that the sessions took place and to find suitable accommodation. The tutors gained in self-esteem. The thinking skills of some tutors observably improved across the curriculum.

Advantages for tutees were thought to be gains in reading and thinking skills and in confidence and self-esteem. Their English teacher reported that they had gained confidence not only in their general reading ability but also in their ability to read aloud in class. Students had also gained in status through having a relationship with a senior student. This had contributed to the perceived gains in self-esteem. The only disadvantage perceived for tutees was that they lost time in some classes in order to participate.

The tutees' English teacher reported that Paired Thinking had raised her expectations of her students, which in turn had raised her confidence in the students' abilities and her own approach to teaching. Paired Thinking had also aided in reinforcing the English curriculum. The principal mathematics teacher highlighted the areas of professional development, cooperation and whole school development. Since she had been responsible for matching the pairs, timetabling the sessions and liaising with staff, she had gained insight into and experience of the theoretical background, techniques and processes involved in implementation of Paired Thinking. Paired Reading had encouraged cooperation among staff as sessions of necessity had to be timetabled across several subjects. Only one change to the implementation was suggested – that those tutees with low reading ability or difficulties with reading be more targeted in the future.

Overall, although both staff and students gave positive evaluations of the process and outcomes, the tutees seemed less enthusiastic about the process than the tutors. How they viewed their random selection for participation might be relevant. Both tutors and staff thought that there had been a positive effect on the thinking skills of both tutors and tutees. Despite their apparently high reading ability, several tutors thought that their reading skills had improved as well as their thinking skills.

Many organizational issues arose. Tutor attrition caused problems, which could be magnified if less committed volunteers were recruited. The long interval between first discussing involvement and the commencement of the program could have led to a decline in motivation for some tutors. Monitoring proved to be problematic at times, as it was not only difficult to locate the pairs, but also logistically difficult to monitor all the pairs due to the different locations and timetables. However, a positive outcome was that tutors spontaneously and of their own volition took on extra tutees in order that no tutee was left without a tutor. This display of motivation and commitment was encouraging not only for the tutees, but also for the staff involved.

Concern is growing in schools regarding the development of transferable skills (such as self-management and working together), and with broader issues such as citizenship education (a component of which is demonstrating care and helping). There is also great interest in improving thinking skills. In a crowded curriculum, it is impossible to create space for such activities without incurring a cost elsewhere. However, the Paired Thinking program, delivered in the format described above, does efficiently combine all those requirements in a very modest allocation of time.

Conclusions and action implications

At the time of writing, it is early days in the evaluation of Paired Thinking, but there is evidence of considerable promise. The action implications for future research and practice are summarized below.

Future research

Clearly more research is needed. Future studies should strive to collect good quality data on implementation integrity, using a range of measures for triangulation purposes and including detailed analysis of actual interactions between tutors and tutees.

Outcome measures of gains in thinking skills need to be considerably more sophisticated, while remaining relevant to the real experiences of the participants. Tests of thinking skills that are individually administered in an interactive context and make no demands on writing skills are preferable. Individual testing may only be possible with a sub-sample, however. Tests must balance the need to avoid a ceiling effect with the need to avoid traumatizing students with completely novel and complex items, especially at post-test. Some form of dynamic assessment which assayed response to graduated prompts would better reflect the PT process. Computer administered tests of thinking skills may offer some interactivity and adaptivity without making demands on writing skills. Any tests used should have reliability and validity pre-established. Additionally, multiple outcome measures should be deployed to triangulate the assessment of thinking gains.

Studies should seek to include control and alternative treatment (with equal time on task) groups. Generalization of thinking skills and longer-term maintenance of gains should be assessed. The operation, effects and durability of Paired Thinking in different formats and contexts needs to be explored, including parents and adult volunteers as well as peers, and in schools and classrooms under stress. Small scale but high quality studies based in a single-site, which are managed and monitored very frequently at close quarters, seem likely to yield more insights than larger studies.

Future practice

If Paired Reading is like learning to ride a bicycle, Paired Thinking seems to be more like re-arranging the furniture (and sometimes making new furniture) – somewhat laborious, if ultimately satisfying, but certainly not a flow experience. Sadly, the better you get at thinking, the harder it becomes, because there is no absolute level of mastery at which you can cruise. Of course, if thinking were easy, people would already be doing it more.

What have we learned about organizing Paired Thinking from these studies?

Format

- What are the advantages and disadvantages of disparate cross-age vs. proximate cross-age peer tutoring?
- What might be the advantages and disadvantages of same-age cross-ability peer tutoring?

- What might be the advantages and disadvantages of same-age same-ability reciprocal peer tutoring?
- Should the questioner/answerer roles be more sharply distinguished, or less sharply?
- In same-age same-ability reciprocal peer tutoring, should these roles rotate per book, per session, per page?

Materials

Access to books needs careful monitoring. Is the system actually working in practice? Does the book supply need changing to fill any emerging gaps, to be more appropriate, or just to refresh the project?

Training

Paired Thinking is more challenging than Paired Reading. It seems clear that from the outset, tutors must be conditioned to expect some cognitive strain, especially younger, less able and near-age tutors. Perhaps PT should be marketed to students as a maturational progression from PR, a more grown-up thing to do.

The minimal training offered is almost certainly too brief to generate high quality practice in all pairs. Further training and/or coaching is likely to be needed, especially with younger, less able and near-age tutors, and especially with non-fiction books. Issues that should be addressed in more detailed training include:

- What exactly might all the prompt questions mean?
- When do you fit in the questions without breaking the flow?
- How exactly do you 'prompt by asking another question'?
- How does the tutor judge if a question is too difficult for their tutee?
- How can PT be made more intrinsically satisfying for tutor and tutee?

Instead of more emphasis on sharply distinguished turn-taking questioner/answerer roles, more emphasis might be placed on thinking aloud (e.g. Baumann *et al.*, 1992). This might create an ethos of exploratory cooperative brainstorming rather than interrogation. However, the mutual understanding and trust necessary for such a development is unlikely to be present in early sessions, and for some pairs might never develop, so the questioning approach probably provides a more durable and widely applicable starting point.

Frequency
- How many sessions per week of what length over what period is optimum?
- What is the optimum duration of PR before moving into PT?
- Would alternating sessions of PR and PT work?

Organization of contact
This will be problematic, especially for cross-age projects and especially in high schools.

- Can tutee and tutor timetables be synchronized?
- Can space for the pair be found, which is reliably available?
- Can access to materials be swift, easy and reliable?
- Can the pairs be easily, regularly and reliably monitored?
- Can staff be reliably and consistently released for training and monitoring?
- Will other commitments or priorities interfere?
- How can the loss of 'regular curricular time' be defended?
- Is it possible to over-spill into personal and social education, recess, club, or other times?

Monitoring
- How can regular and frequent monitoring be sustained?
- Do tutors need extrinsic and/or extra social reinforcement?

Evaluation
- How can generalization to reading and thinking across the curriculum be ensured?
- How can generalization to reading and thinking across the curriculum be measured?

It seems appropriate that this chapter on Paired Thinking ends with more questions than answers.

9 How To Evaluate Paired Thinking

Paired Thinking is a relatively new development and much more evaluation is needed. Its durability in many different contexts, including schools and classrooms under stress, should be explored. Relative effectiveness with parent and volunteer tutors as well as peers needs to be investigated.

Chapter 8 noted the desirability of research into Paired Thinking that included control groups, and preferably also comparison alternative treatment groups involving equal time on task. Generalization of thinking skills should ideally be assessed, as should the longer-term maintenance of any gains. However, this is the work of many people over many years. Do not expect to manage all of this in your first project.

The discussion of research designs and methods for Paired Reading applies here also (reading Chapter 5 before this chapter will be very helpful). Measures will of course be different.

As with all evaluation, this should be conducted with reference to the objectives set for the project, which may be academic, affective, social, or a combination of these.

Implementation process

In Chapter 8 the need for further research on Paired Thinking to be conducted very carefully at close quarters was noted. As PT is relatively new, it is particularly important that evidence of the quality of implementation is gathered in any evaluations. This will guide possible future adaptations to and developments of the method. Equally importantly, future reports of outcomes need to be seen in the context of whether PT was delivered and carried out properly by the participants.

Chapter 5 explores these issues in relation to PR, and much of this is relevant to PT. Process observations collected using the PT Technique Checklist (see TRW website) should be systematically analysed as part of any evaluation. Direct observation, video and/or audio recording, semi-structured interviews with different types of participants, and various forms of ethnographic data collection should help to give multiple perspectives on implementation fidelity.

Problems of outcome measurement

Measurement of quality of thinking is problematic. The main practical problem is finding measures of thinking abilities that are accessible to young children, reliable and valid, sensitive to short-term gains, and also economical in time for administration and scoring and in purchase cost. Unsurprisingly, there is no right way to do it.

Using more than one outcome measure is recommended to triangulate the assessment of gains in thinking skills. In an area where measurement is difficult, the use of multiple measures of independent imperfection is a wise strategy.

Royer (1993) reviewed a range of procedures useful in assessing enhancement of cognitive skills. A more useful resource for the practitioner is the book by Norris and Ennis (1989). This discusses a wide range of classroom-based criterion-referenced quality indicator measures and commercially available critical thinking tests.

The hazy borderline between higher order reading skills and thinking skills is another complication. The literature suggests results on tests of reading comprehension and thinking abilities tend to be highly correlated across large numbers of students. However, you are likely to be working with a small and atypical group. In any event, how could you interpret such a correlation? The most able students tend to do well on most tests. This does not mean that causality can be assumed for any particular linkage.

The other problem here is that many brief reading comprehension tests do not actually test higher order reading skills, but only the ability to remember information presented in the test items, which are often brief and de-contextualized. While selecting the correct information might require some thought, this task could hardly be considered to be assessing critical thinking skills in any generalized way. Student motivation to apply higher order thinking skills to such test items might also be a factor.

An especially critical question is how generalization to reading and thinking across the curriculum can be promoted and ensured, and correspondingly how this could be measured.

Norm-referenced tests

If thinking skills programs make kids smarter, why not evaluate with IQ tests on a before and after basis?

Many traditional intelligence tests would be a very severe test of generalization of a short program designed to improve thinking skills. Many intelligence tests were specifically designed to measure innate intelligence, by definition not affected by environmental events like education (although this no longer seems plausible). Indeed, many IQ tests have been criticized for cultural bias, and are increasingly in disrepute as the conception of intelligence becomes less singular and much wider.

Also, intelligence tests typically present abstract de-contextualized test items, which seem likely to favor students who have been involved in thinking skills programs of the abstract additive kind, but not students who have experienced infusion subject-based thinking skills programs, nor indeed those based in transferable skills (like PT).

What are the options in norm-referenced tests of thinking skills? Unfortunately, there are not too many that are likely to be reliable and valid for this purpose. Apart from intelligence tests, there are many fewer standardized tests of thinking than of reading, and in many countries there are no standardized tests available in the first language of the country. Where standardized tests are available, they vary greatly from country to country. Virtually none of the tests used in the UK are used in the US, and vice versa.

Norris and Ennis (1989) discuss a range of commercially available critical thinking tests, but many of these are targeted at older students. For example, Robert Ennis himself (with Jason Millman) has developed the Cornell Critical Thinking Tests. Level X of these tests is targeted at grade 5 through college, while Level Z is aimed at advanced secondary (available from Critical Thinking Press and Software, www.criticalthinking.com).

Norm-referenced tests of thinking skills are not without their structural problems. For instance, Jacobs (1999) researched the equivalence of the parallel forms A and B of the California Critical Thinking Skills Test, and found low reliability in terms of internal consistency, a lack of comparability between the forms, and poor construct validity.

One of the few norm-referenced tests applicable to elementary school students is the Ross Test of Higher Cognitive Processes (Ross and Ross, 1976). This is said to be designed to access the higher-level thinking skills of both gifted and non-gifted students in grades four through six, but seems to require considerable reading skill and a highly systematic approach to the test. It requires two hour-long sessions for group administration and is very demanding for the children.

Those wishing to use norm-referenced tests of thinking skills should scrutinize the catalogs of the major educational test suppliers in their country (most of which are now available on-line) for more up-to-date offerings. Alternatively, access more general compendiums of tests, such as the Buros database of mental measurements (also now available on-line). The latter reports on freely available public domain tests as well as commercially available tests. In either case, you need to look for substantial evidence of reliability and validity in real-life field applications such as your project.

Criterion-referenced assessment

Stiggins *et al.* (1989) describe a variety of ways of measuring thinking skills through classroom assessment. Norris and Ennis (1989) discuss a wide range of classroom-based criterion-referenced quality indicator measures.

Curriculum-based continuous prose Cloze procedure group tests of reading comprehension have been noted in the literature to be particularly sensitive to short-term pre–post experimental effects from projects of this kind. However, to what extent this extends the evaluation beyond reading comprehension and into thinking is debatable.

Curriculum-based and criterion-referenced reading and thinking tests can be devised, based on standardized reading passages that are

likely to be motivating and culturally appropriate for the participants. (This is the approach adopted in the Bryce project, discussed
in Chapter 8). The assessor works with children individually, doing
Paired Reading with the standardized texts, then asking the participants Paired Thinking questions (from the same Level appropriate to
the participant on both occasions).

If no control group is available for testing, the standard texts need
to be of equivalent readability (and equivalent comprehensibility) at
pre-test and post-test. If parallel control group scores are available,
equivalent readability is less of an issue, as the experimental change
can be directly compared to the control change. Ideally, each participant's responses would be audio recorded at both pre-test and post-
test, then rated for intellectual quality by two separate raters. How
that rating scale is constructed is another thorny issue.

Following from the above, a Reading Summarization Test might
be constructed. Participants could be asked to summarize standard
passages (or even whole short books of comparable readability) at
pre-test and post-test (responding orally or in writing or both), and
the cognitive quality of these summaries rated by experts.

However, such measures invite many questions:

- Are the criteria clearly and precisely articulated?
- Are the criteria widely accepted, or idiosyncratic to their
  creator?
- Are they based on empirical research?
- Are they unambiguous and capable of yielding high inter-
  rater reliabilities?
- How 'objective' can the assessment of thinking ever be?
- What if the child to be assessed is a lot smarter than the
  assessor?

Paris (1991) discussed the assessment of meta-cognitive aspects of
reading comprehension. Measures such as his Index of Reading
Awareness were found to have low reliability and validity, perhaps
partially because meta-cognitive functioning probably accounts for
only a modest proportion of the total variance in reading performance.

Van Kraayenoord and Paris (1997) describe the meta-cognitive interview – a structured means of accessing a student's insight into his or her own learning processes – which they used with students in the fourth through sixth grade. The scope of this tool was considerably broader than thinking skills, but a more focussed meta-cognitive thinking skills interview schedule could be developed. The Meta-cognitive Interview is similar to the Reading Interview, in which students are asked specifically about their insights into their own reading strategies. Such interviews could be used on a pre-test and post-test basis, with some analysis of categorical changes over the period.

Other possible measures

Other measures more specific to Paired Thinking could be used:

- Knowledge Test – students could be given some kind of test of their superficial knowledge of the strategies encompassed within the PT method in which they have been trained.
- Questioning Fluency Assessment – participants could be asked to generate questions (a quiz) about standard passages, (although such a procedure did not yield positive results in studies of the Reciprocal Teaching method).
- Prediction Fluency Assessment – students could be stopped at standard points in a standard story, and asked to make predictions.
- Behavior Recording – the dialogue between children could be directly observed and/or audio recorded and/or video recorded during sampled activity sessions, on a pre–post basis before, during and after a PT project. Changes in their behavior and the cognitive quality of that behavior would then be analysed with reference to a structured observation schedule. This would be a process as well as an outcome measure. The same method could be used to investigate generalization to thinking outside the PT sessions.
- Think-Aloud Content Analysis – specimen 'think-alouds', perhaps in relation to a standard task, could be recorded on a pre–post basis and their (hopefully improving) quality

assessed. Tutors and tutees could be separate or together or both.

Self-concept and attitude

In Chapter 5 the paucity of reliable and valid measures of self-concept as a reader that could be used with young children was noted. Parallel measures of self-concept as a thinker are even harder to find. Trawling existing generic self-concept scales for items relevant to this focus could form a basis for developing your own measure.

Subjective feedback

Specimen Paired Thinking Evaluation Questionnaires are available (on the TRW website) to gather feedback in a standardized way from participants. Questionnaires suitable for tutees, tutors and teachers are provided. These give all participants an equal opportunity to contribute (unless the reading skills of some are below the readability level of the questionnaire).

Paired Thinking can operate with a wide age range of students, and a large number of rather difficult questions are included in the questionnaires for tutors and tutees. Depending on the nature of your participants, you may wish to delete some of the items of lesser interest or relevance, and reword others to lower the readability level. The questions could also inform the creation of a semi-structured interview schedule for any of the participants.

Group and individual feedback interviews with tutors and tutees and other relevant participants would offer general insights within a semi-structured framework. Interviews are more time-consuming than questionnaires, and therefore often completed only with a sample carefully selected to be genuinely representative of all participants. However, interviews permit follow-up questioning, and responses are likely to be less superficial than to a questionnaire, unless the interviewer is in a position of power in relation to the interviewee.

As described in Chapter 8, some schools conduct a pre- and post-Circle Time with participants (tutors in one circle and tutees in another). This could be video or audio recorded (permitting later content analysis if the quality is satisfactory). Circle Time has the advantage of a trusting and familiar context and empowerment of all children to contribute their opinions. It may have the disadvantage of group contamination, early responses leading other students to imitate rather than think for themselves. Later students might also have reservations about publicly voicing an opinion that disagrees with the majority view which has by then emerged.

Please let the author know of any further means for measuring the development of thinking skills that you have tried out in your context, especially if they proved successful within the limited time and resources available.

Part Three
Paired Writing

10 What Is Paired Writing?

> If the work is difficult, [The Writer] feels alone and some-
> times even abandoned. But ... that which is named loneli-
> ness is probably more nearly ineffectiveness, a form of
> failure, or form of fear ...   *William Saroyan*

> Collaborative writing is the key to unlocking the silences of
> children   *E. S. Fine*

The notion that writing, like reading, must have a life, application,
purposes and audiences beyond class work and indeed beyond
school is now a mainstream idea.

Paired Writing is a useful tool in this developmental process. It is a
system for peer, parent or volunteer tutoring (or co-composition) of
any sort of writing (creative or technical) in any language.

Poor or beginning or challenged writers are most likely to have
difficulties in ideas generation, text organization and meta-cognitive
knowledge of the writing process (Englert and Raphael, 1988). We
are all challenged writers when attempting a type or format of writing or a writing topic or a level of critical analysis which is new to us.
Paired Writing specifically supports these aspects. It is not, of course,
just for poor writers.

Paired Writing is similar to Paired Reading. It is a framework and
set of guidelines to be followed by pairs working together to generate a piece of writing for a purpose. It gives a supportive structure to
scaffold interactive collaborative behaviors through all stages of the
writing process.

Like the other methods in this book, it is a clearly structured and
specific method. It contains little new, but elaborates standard and
widely accepted elements of process writing, regularizing them systematically into a cohesive method. Paired Writing should not be
confused with other similarly named methods, or with various

shared writing methods that have been reported (but not apparently rigorously evaluated).

The assumption of Paired Writing is that two individuals produce better quality writing together than they each would if working separately. Writing is about the communication of thoughts, so to produce a greater quantity of writing is not necessarily better. It is the quality that counts in effective communication.

Design parameters for Paired Writing

The emphasis in Paired Writing (PW) is on thinking, planning, intelligent questioning, self-disclosure and discussion, reorganization and restructuring – to counterbalance the traditional focus on mechanics and the final product.

The framework and the interaction between the pair are also designed to result in a higher proportion of time actually spent on-task, reducing to a minimum head-scratching, dithering, staring out of the window and blind panic at the sight of a blank piece of paper.

There is a great emphasis on continuity, the pair stimulating each other to keep going at any threatened hiatus. There is also a great deal of in-built constant feedback and cross-checking – what is written must make sense to both members of the pair. Partners offer a continuous sense of audience and almost immediate feedback. The clear role division of labor at every stage in the PW framework helps to modulate information processing, promote flow and reduce anxiety.

The system is designed to be supportive and eliminate the fear of failure. Anxiety about peripheral aspects of writing such as spelling and punctuation should be reduced to an appropriate level, and dealt with in an orderly way. As the best copy is a joint effort of the pair, criticism as well as praise from external evaluators is shared.

Peer evaluation is incorporated, relieving the supervising professional of the burden of marking or grading innumerable scripts after the event (sometimes so long after, that the feedback given is totally ineffective in improving subsequent efforts). Research shows that peer evaluation is at least as effective as teacher evaluation.

The professionals involved have a broad organizational role. They need to train the pairs, monitor subsequent practice to ensure the system is being used properly, and be on hand to help resolve any problems as well as to give praise.

The pairs can be children working with other children in school, parents working with their own children at home, or non-professional volunteers working with children in school. Adults needing help with basic literacy also recruit pair support from spouses, parents, children, friends, neighbors and work colleagues, and do Paired Writing at home, at work or elsewhere. Sometimes adults attending basic literacy classes do Paired Writing on a peer tutor basis in the class itself.

Paired Writing is usually operated in pairs where one member (the Helper) is more skilful at writing than the other (the Writer). In this case, the method is usually targeted on writing tasks somewhat beyond the current independent writing competence of the less able partner, but within their zone of proximal development.

However, the system is durable and a differential in writing skill in the pair is not essential so long as the pair edit carefully and use a dictionary to check spelling. Paired Writing on a same-ability basis may maximize mutual interest and respect and permit reciprocation of roles on alternating writing tasks to increase novelty.

The system may be used in creative writing or English composition, or in descriptive or technical writing (e.g. writing up a science experiment or field trip) or as part of cross-curricular project work. It can also be used as part of foreign language teaching.

A Paired Writing project may be designed to mesh with, and follow on from, direct instruction from a professional teacher on structural aspects of the writing process such as grammar. However, it may equally be operated on an ad hoc basis as the need arises, once pairs are trained and practiced in its use.

Frequency of usage of Paired Writing need not be prescribed for a certain number of weeks. During the week or two immediately after training, it is important that pairs use the system from beginning to end at least three times to consolidate their practice and become fluent in the method. After this, the frequency of usage may vary greatly from pair to pair according to their own situation and purposes. Teachers may still choose to prescribe an initial intensive commitment period with some groups.

PW is designed to promote a sense of participant ownership of a learner-managed process, not least to help avoid feelings of helplessness and dependency. Of course, it is intended to have effects beyond the particular writing task the pair are working on. Generalized effects to subsequent individual writing for both participants are sought (except perhaps where the ability differential between partners is very large).

The Paired Writing system

At first sight, the Paired Writing system might seem rather complicated. Don't be put off. You can train many seven-year-olds to do it in two half-hour sessions – it is a lot simpler than it looks.

Paired Writing consists of:

6 STEPS	
+	
10 Questions	(Ideas)
5 Stages	(Drafting)
4 Levels	(Editing)

The Paired Writing Flowchart outlines the system (see the TRW website). A copy of this flowchart is provided to each pair for initial training and subsequent reference. It would be helpful to refer to this flowchart as you read this section. (Each section of the flowchart is also provided in large format as an overhead master.)

Within the flowchart, note the terminology: 'Helper' is the tutor, 'Writer' is the tutee.

Step 1 Ideas generation

The Helper stimulates ideas by raising the stimulus words listed under Questions (Who? Do? What? To? With? Where? When? How? Why?) with the Writer, not necessarily in the order listed. These are nine of the ten Ideas Questions. (The tenth question is a blank or wild card option to indicate that Helpers can think up their own.)

The flowchart also indicates a What Next loop with a further four suggested conjunction Questions (Then? And? If? But?) which the Helper may wish to use.

Helpers are expected to think about which of these questions are relevant to the task in hand and to where the Writer is starting from. Helpers are expected to present the given questions in a strategic order, not just mechanically in the order they appear on the flowchart. Helpers are also expected to think of other more relevant (but brief) questions or new stimulus words themselves as ideas develop.

As the Writer responds verbally, the Helper makes one-word rough notes to help the pair remember the Ideas (two words at most). As this proceeds, the Helper may revisit previous questions and/or recapitulate previous ideas before presenting the next stimulus word.

Mapping

It is most unlikely that the Ideas will be verbalized in exactly the right or best organized order straight away. Before moving on to the next step, it is helpful for the pair to review the Ideas notes, and discuss and try to map the relationships between them. These relationships may be simply temporal, concerning the best order in which to present the Ideas, or other relationships between Ideas might be considered.

This mapping can be indicated simply by numbering the Ideas in order. Alternatively, the Ideas may seem to fall into obvious sections, which can be dealt with in turn. Such sections could be color-coded and Ideas belonging to them underlined with a colored pencil. Pairs may also choose to draw lines linking or around related Ideas, so that a semantic map is constructed. Other expressions which have been used for organizing ideas in this way include mind maps, word webs, skeleton plans, clustering, and so on. All of these are very valuable ways of organizing Ideas before rushing on to writing continuously. All of them make the pair really think.

You may feel that mapping deserves to be a step in its own right, and of course you could adapt the flowchart along these lines if you wish. Alternatively, you might feel that the flowchart is already large and complex enough (especially at first sight).

Step 2 Drafting

The rough and brief Ideas notes should be placed where both members of the pair can easily see them. Drafting then proceeds. The sequence of the content is put down in continuous prose. This is done without concern for spelling, punctuation or grammatical perfection. Legibility is desirable, however, as is double-spaced writing to allow for subsequent editing. Most pairs will do better with lined paper and pencils rather than pens.

The Writer considers the notes and dictates, sentence by sentence, what he or she wishes to communicate. Which of the pair actually writes this down is governed by their choice of one of the five Drafting Support Stages (see the flowchart):

1. Helper writes it all in rough, Writer copies it all
2. Helper writes difficult words for Writer
3. Helper writes difficult words in rough for Writer to write
4. Helper dictates how to write difficult words
5. Writer writes it all

The pair may choose a stage to apply to the whole session or just to a small section of the task (perhaps even only one word). For a harder piece of writing, they are likely to choose a low (numbered) stage, for an easier assignment a high (numbered) stage. Thus support varies with task difficulty and Writer competence. The pair do need to make a definite decision to start off; this can always be amended later if necessary.

However, they may go back one stage (or more) when encountering a particularly hard bit. In any event, if the Writer can't proceed within ten seconds, the Helper must go back a stage on that problem word to give more support. There is great emphasis on keeping going and maintaining the flow. Keeping going with more support is much better than struggling for a long time with less support.

An additional help sheet outlining the Drafting Support Stages is provided on the TRW website. You may wish to look at this now. Use this carefully with pairs. Do not drown them in too much paper too early.

Step 3 Reading

The Helper then reads the draft out loud, with as much expression and attention to punctuation as possible, while the Helper and the Writer look at the text together. The Writer then follows this example. If the Writer reads a word incorrectly, the Helper immediately says that word correctly.

Some pairs like to repeat this Step after Step 4 Editing. An alternative permutation might be to have the Writer only reading at Step 3 and the Helper only repeat reading after Step 4.

Step 4 Editing

Helper and Writer look at the draft together, and the Writer considers where he or she thinks improvements are necessary. The problem words, phrases or sentences may be marked with another colored pen, pencil or highlighter.

There are four suggested criteria for assessment of the draft, the four Edit Levels.

The most important criterion of need for improvement is where Meaning is unclear. The second most important is to do with the organization of the separate ideas in the text, or the Order in which meanings are presented. This could refer to organization within a phrase or sentence, or organization of the order of sentences.

The next consideration is whether Spellings are correct, and the last whether Punctuation is helpful and correct. Some Writers may wish to inspect the draft four times, checking with reference to a different criterion on each occasion, especially when they are first learning to use the system.

The Helper praises the Writer for completion of this demanding task, then points out any areas or problems the Writer has missed, while bearing in mind the subjective nature of some aspects of quality in writing.

The pair discuss the best corrections to make. The Writer can then make any additional suggestions about changes. When agreement is reached the new version is inserted in the text (preferably by the Writer). Spellings over which there is the slightest doubt should be checked in a dictionary.

An additional Editing and Evolution Reminder sheet is provided on the TRW website. You may wish to look at this now.

Step 5 Best copy

The Writer then usually copies out a neat or best version of the corrected draft. Sometimes the Helper may write or keyboard the piece, depending on the skill and stamina levels of the Writer. There is no reason why members of the pair could not take turns to write sections of the best copy, to share the boredom. Indeed, another scribe could take over the task completely.

The actual physical act of writing is considered the least important step in Paired Writing, so it does not really matter who does it. The important thing is the quality of thinking and communication in the process. The best copy is a joint product of the pair. It follows that both should have their names on it. Photocopying enables each member of the pair to have a copy.

Step 6 Evaluate

The pair should then inspect, consider and assess the best copy. Given the effort they have jointly expended, they are likely to think their co-composed text is really rather good and be happy to congratulate each other as members of a successful team of two (or composing duet).

However, external evaluation by assessors less likely to be wearing rose-tinted spectacles is also highly desirable. Peer evaluation is a useful mutual learning experience. Assessment by another pair is probably best, and can proceed by reference to the criteria encompassed in the Edit Levels.

An additional Editing and Evaluation Reminder sheet is provided on the TRW website. You may wish to look at this now. However, use this carefully with pairs. Do not drown them in too much paper too early.

Where Paired Writing occurs between children in a school setting, the first two pairs to finish can exchange best copies for mutual evaluation. This should temper any inclination to be over-critical. Positive evaluative comments must outnumber non-positive comments, and non-positive comments should be expressed in overtly subjective and sensitive terms.

This involvement in the evaluation of the work of others is of course intended to improve the self-evaluation skills of both members of each pair. These skills should then transfer to new situations, including those when the Writer is writing alone.

You will also find on the TRW website PW Self and Peer Evaluation Forms, encouraging participants to reflect upon their role and performance in the PW process, and their contribution to the quality of the finished product. However, use this carefully with pairs – do not overwhelm them with paper.

Feedback and praise

Project organizers should also emphasize that there are not necessarily any right answers about what constitutes good writing. Helpers should avoid direct criticism of the Writer's efforts, but instead make comments about their own subjective reaction, e.g. 'I find that bit hard to understand. Can we think of a clearer way to write it?' Modeling this in training meetings is helpful.

Helpers (and evaluators) must praise good bits more than they draw attention to problems, e.g. 'That's an interesting word', 'I like the way you put that, it's really clear.' Praise should be given at the end of each step. Praise points are indicated on the flowchart.

A linear or recursive process?

Especially during reciprocal tutoring, the Helper and Writer roles may blur to some extent. Such blurring is no bad thing if it counteracts any tendency for Helpers to become overly didactic. However, do not let roles slip too far or the pair will degenerate into confusion or, worse still, argument. Each should be and remain clear about their job description. Emphasize that 'Helpers are to help Writers to help themselves, not do everything for them.'

The flowchart of the Paired Writing system is linear for ease of immediate understanding. However, early conceptions of the writing process as a series of sequential steps have been moderated by more organic or holistic models, in which any component of the writing process may repeat and overlap with, link to, or incorporate any other. Educators have increasingly emphasized recursive components of the writing process, which communicate with, feed back to, and interrupt each other at various points (e.g. Scardamalia and Bereiter, 1986). The shift to hypertextual rather than textual models of literacy also seems in conflict with linear conceptions of the writing process.

Additionally, some children, given the opportunity but no training, will spontaneously engage in collaborative interaction of various sorts while writing, as Schultz (1997) and others have noted. However, not all learners may be able to do this, especially in less favorable contexts or circumstances. For the teacher, the problem of how to instruct such learners in complex interactions is substantial, as is that of monitoring the quality of subsequent activity. Teachers, tutors and tutees have to start somewhere – a particular issue with younger or less able children, with classes inexperienced in collaborative methods, with classes under other stresses, and with teachers who just don't have a whole lot of time to spare. Also, process writing has to be available to all on an equal opportunity basis.

The linear PW model is already complex, at first sight. Perhaps linearity at the point of introduction is not the problem, but a failure to subsequently move children on to anything more complex and recursive. Once pairs are more familiar with the elements of the linear model, it is likely that their procedure will diversify and begin to incorporate recursive loops between steps. The first of these is often the introduction of additional reading of some or all of the draft at another step.

Once children are competent with the method and integrating it more freely into everyday writing, teachers need to monitor which children are spontaneously beginning to use the elements of the method recursively, and which need further encouragement to do so. Otherwise there may be a danger of a few children becoming fixed, rigid, mechanistic and rule-bound in their operation of the method.

Recursive adaptations are often effective, but are not necessarily so. They may also have the side-effect of extending the time taken and leaving insufficient time for the adequate completion of later steps. Remember the Paired Writing structure is also intended to help children successfully complete more pieces of writing, and thus experience the later stages of the process as frequently and fully as the earlier ones. Pairs should be encouraged to think carefully about the effectiveness of their adaptations to the basic method, and project organizers should monitor this aspect of Paired Writing.

Additional elements

Additions and/or adaptations can also be made to the system to render it more suitable for particular circumstances.

For instance, Paired Writing can be linked with Cued Spelling (see Part Four), to ensure Writers have a minimal level of skill in the accurate and swift free writing of high frequency words.

At Step 3 Read, the full Paired Reading technique (see Part One) could be used if necessary or desirable by those pairs familiar with it.

At Step 4 Edit, additional editing levels could be included to extend the complexity and depth of analysis of the draft. This may be particularly desirable with more sophisticated participants, especially when generating creative writing.

Thus, for instance, a Level 1a Wording could be introduced to encourage pairs to deploy more interesting, varied and precise vocabulary. A Level 2a Grammar could be concerned with syntactical structure. If considered important, a Level 3a Capitalization could be introduced. Level 4 Punctuation could also be taken to include paragraphing. Equally, a Level 5a Handwriting could be introduced, to encourage Pairs to improve legibility and formation of the handwriting of best copy as well as general presentation. Beware too great an emphasis on mechanics, however, or your pairs will start to dislike Paired Writing.

More subtle Edit Levels might include:

5b Purpose (considering appropriateness for aims and audience specified),
5c Ideas Quality (considering originality and creativity),
5d Focus (considering semantic density, repetition and redundancy).

However, take care not to make the system too complex too soon, or pairs will increasingly depart from it or begin to skip sections.

These possible elaborations on the basic Edit Levels are listed below:

Edit Levels
1. MEANING   1a Wording
2. ORDER   2a Grammar
3. SPELLING   3a Capitalization
4. PUNCTUATION   4a Paragraphing
5. OTHER   5a Handwriting
                    5b Purpose
                    5c Ideas Quality
                    5d Focus

The additional Edit Levels may also be used in Step 6 Evaluate, or perhaps be used only in Step 6.

Other permutations and applications readily present themselves. For novelty, pairs might alternate roles during Step 1 Ideas even during a single session, so each member of the pair is thinker and stimulator-recorder in turn, particularly if the pair is writing fiction.

It may be possible to operate Paired Writing directly on a computer, which could prove much swifter. However, consideration would have to be given to how the pair could mark or flag those parts of the text they wished to edit.

Remember that Paired Writing is co-composition – both members of the pair own the finished product. If copies have to be submitted individually for further external assessment or inclusion in a portfolio of achievements, each member of the pair should have a copy.

Conclusion

Obviously, the Paired Writing method is only one of many possible ways in which collaborative writing could be structured and scaffolded. However, it is a clear and carefully designed framework, which includes many elements already acknowledged as desirable in the research literature, in classroom practice, and in national curricular prescriptions. Importantly, it has been shown to be practical, flexible, robust and effective. Furthermore, it requires virtually no new materials or other expenditure. Thus it might help to encourage innovation for teachers uncertain where and how to start, and provide a useful basis for progression and development.

Given the increasing accuracy and accessibility of computer speech recognition, the best copy stage of writing can be expected to become increasingly automated. Several other stages of the Paired Writing method may prove efficiently operable in a computer-assisted writing environment (e.g. MacArthur, 1999). Collaborative writing between partners in different countries through the Internet could be scaffolded through the Paired Writing framework. The possibilities for classroom-based action research are many.

11 How To Organize Paired Writing

Paired Writing projects follow many of the organizational guidelines for Paired Reading projects (reading Chapter 3 before this chapter is very helpful).

You will be able to use much of the PR parent and peer tutoring Planning Proformas (see TRW website) in planning a Paired Writing project. Similar organizational questions must be answered about context and objectives, recruitment, selection and matching, training, organization of contact, support and monitoring, feedback, and evaluation. One planning area which is very different is, of course, Materials. In what follows, repetition will be avoided as far as possible, emphasis being given to significant organizational differences for Paired Writing as compared to PR.

The context and objectives for a Paired Writing project must be considered carefully. Is Paired Writing to be targeted on many types of writing for many purposes, or just one? Starting with a restricted focus would be prudent, especially if the work can be organized and monitored by one or two enthusiastic teachers. Given success in a restricted initiative, the method can gradually be spread to other types of writing, other areas of the curriculum, other places, other purposes and audiences, and other professional supervisors.

Recruitment, selection and matching

Many of the considerations from recruitment, selection and matching in Paired Reading apply (see Chapter 3). Paired Writing is often used on a peer tutoring basis, but equally lends itself to parent and volunteer tutoring.

Peer tutoring can be with pairs of the same age (often within the same class, which makes organization much easier) or of different ages. Where there is a differential in writing ability in the pair, it should not be too great. Otherwise, the Helper (tutor) may become bored and/or dominant and the Writer (tutee) insecure and/or dependent, especially if they are fixed in these roles and Paired Writing goes on for a long time.

In order to match up pairs, class teachers rank order their children according to estimated writing ability. For cross-ability projects, this list is then divided into the most able half (Helpers) and the less able (Writers), the most able Helper paired with the most able Writer, and so on by parallel matching. This avoids too great a writing differential between partners. For same-ability projects, the most able participant is paired with the next most able, and so on down the list.

Personality is the second matching consideration, since potential conflict should be avoided. Be careful when matching personality types who are very similar or very dissimilar. Teachers usually avoid putting best friends or worst enemies together, unless they are absolutely sure they will work well. This is perhaps more important with Paired Writing than with the other paired methods. Gender is usually not considered, although it may become significant if participants are to have a completely free choice of writing topics, and the Writer has very narrow and fixed interests.

If pairs are matched to be of similar writing skill, you may choose to operate reciprocal tutoring. In this case, the roles of Writer and Helper are best alternated after the completion of each piece of writing.

In the case of parent and volunteer tutoring, a large differential in writing ability between Helper and Writer is more likely (but not necessarily so, if the Writer is a high school student, or the parental competence in writing is not great).

Materials

Each pair must have a system flowchart (on the TRW website), two pens or pencils, rough paper for drafting, easy access to a dictionary, and good quality paper for a best copy. Colored pens, pencils or highlighters for editing are helpful. Consider whether to prescribe lined paper and/or forbid erasers. It is strongly recommended that the use of erasers be heavily discouraged. Supervising professionals may decide whether lined or unlined paper is appropriate for each pair on an individual basis.

If you have chosen to introduce the PW method in two shorter training sessions rather than one long one, you will need printed copies of the flowchart divided into sections accordingly.

Consider which of the optional PW help sheets (on the TRW website) might be useful to your tutors and tutees (PW Drafting Support Stages, Editing and Evaluation Reminder Sheet, Self and Peer Evaluation Forms). Also consider carefully when the chosen sheets should be distributed, to whom, and in what order. Do not drown participants in too much paper.

Entry skills

Writers should minimally be able to:

- define a sentence
- read the flowchart and their draft
- write legibly
- write letter sounds and/or names to dictation, although this could be taught as a parallel exercise.

Helpers should minimally have:

- adequate receptive and expressive language
- the ability to write relatively simple single words legibly
- the ability to read continuous prose at the appropriate level, preferably with a degree of expression
- some minimal competence in spelling and punctuation
- the ability to use a simple dictionary (although this could be taught as a parallel exercise).

Training

Pairs must be properly trained in the use of the system. Hold a training session at which participants sit in their pairs at tables with the required materials at hand. Describe the system, referring to the flowchart. Each pair must have a print copy of the flowchart during the training session, which they will keep for subsequent reference. You may also wish to show the chart on an overhead projector in enlarged sections (see PW Method Overhead Masters on TRW website).

Demonstrating Paired Writing involves the audience in seeing a lot of intricate written detail as well as listening carefully to the discussions of the model pair. If you use video modeling, the video will have to be very carefully made. Role play between two teachers (or maybe between a teacher and a robust, confident child with a loud voice) is the easiest way. Deliberate mistakes are made to show correction procedures. (Note that the Paired Writing video listed on the TRW website is a demonstration of a training session, not material to be used for demonstration in a training session.)

Immediate practice for all pairs follows. Choose a very brief and self-contained writing task for the demonstration, such as writing some instructions for an everyday task. The pair can operate standing by an overhead projector and use this to show what they are writing at each stage. Prepared lined acetate sheets are a good idea. The demonstrating pair need to ensure that deliberate mistakes are made at Ideas and Draft stages, to show how writers are supported through these.

To allow every practicing pair to think up their own topic for practice would be unmanageable. Specify a very brief and self-contained information writing task which is common to the experience of all pairs. Writing some simple instructions usually works well, and some humor often results. Examples are: 'How To Tie Your Shoelaces' or 'How To Brush Your Teeth'. Keep it very simple. Everything turns out much more complicated and time-consuming than you imagined.

While the pairs practice, you circulate to monitor technique. The Paired Writing Technique Checklist (see TRW website) will be helpful for this. Emphasize that Helpers should not be too directive or too helpful.

Allow at least an hour for the whole training session. Alternatively (especially with younger Writers), you may prefer to divide the training into two sessions, to consolidate the first two Steps before introducing the rest. The two sessions should not be more than a day or two apart.

Young children may tend to be very concrete and rule-bound, perhaps for example following the prompt questions in Step 1 in the listed order, rather than reflecting on the current relevance of each to the task in hand. In Step 2, some participants may have difficulty with the vocabulary and concepts of the stages of support, and further demonstrations and explanations can prove necessary (see Drafting Support Stages help sheet on the TRW website).

Where more complex Edit Levels are used, further training of pairs will be necessary. This is usually best done as a later development once the basic system has been understood and experienced for some time. A sample of writing can be displayed on the overhead projector and·edited as a whole group exercise. Pairs can then practice editing samples of their own past writing before embarking on full Paired Writing.

Contact organization

In the two weeks after training, the system will need to be used as frequently as possible, to ensure consolidation, promote fluency and enable any problems to be detected and corrected. Subsequently less frequent use is possible, according to needs.

Normally teachers schedule peer tutor Paired Writing for specific sessions within the regular scheduled Language Arts or English curriculum to start with. Once established, Paired Writing can be extended into other curriculum time slots for other purposes, e.g. into science and technology for recording and reporting. As Paired Writing is increasingly implemented across the curriculum, less and less Language Arts time need be allocated for this purpose.

In peer tutor projects, if one member of a pair is absent from school, teachers either rematch the children, or have them write individually for that session. Pairs will progress at different rates, and teachers often have further writing activities discretely available for early finishers. Especially when the method is new to them, slower pairs will be at risk of not completing all stages (especially the last, peer evaluation) within the time available, and will need teacher support with time management. One or two pairs may tend to omit other steps, intentionally or otherwise.

With peer-tutored Paired Writing in class, practical problems include varied time requirements and noise levels. However, you would hope for some spontaneous generalization of the procedure to preparation, homework, break or recess, or even leisure time. Should this occur, the problem of time requirements will diminish.

You may wish to promote this generalization by offering facilities for a Writer's Club to meet at lunch time. Certainly you should let the participants know that you are seeking this generalization and are prepared to encourage it in any practical way you can.

Also emphasize that co-composition through Paired Writing is not cheating. But take care that the participants do not generalize the method to the written homework requirements of other teachers who may regard it as cheating. Discussion with colleagues is necessary.

When Paired Writing is used in open community settings (e.g. with parents and children or adult-to-adult), an informal contract regarding minimum frequency of usage could be established – e.g. Paired Writing for three sessions of twenty minutes per week for six weeks. This initial prescription is necessary to establish fluency and positive habits, particularly in previously reluctant writers. After this period, participants can review for themselves how they wish to proceed.

Support, monitoring and feedback

Self-monitoring is a major feature of Paired Writing. However, pairs still need some external monitoring and support especially in the early stages.

Direct observation during peer tutor Paired Writing sessions or during booster meetings for parent or volunteer tutor projects is essential to check conformity to technique and advise on any necessary adaptations for individual pairs. Take care not to be drawn into commenting on apparent quality of output when monitoring conformity to technique. This is in the first instance the task and responsibility of the pair. The monitor is supervising process, not product. A Teacher Peer Tutoring Role Reminder Sheet is available on the TRW website to help monitors.

The Editing Step needs especially careful checking for quality, to ensure the primary focus is really on meaning and order, and not on spelling and punctuation. The quantity and quality of discussion can be expected to improve once the children have become familiar with the structure. Monitors should encourage and stimulate discussion (even at the expense of raised noise levels).

Where educators prefer to try out Paired Writing in the cross-ability format first, a warning will be needed for cross-ability Helpers that their gains may be meta-cognitive and somewhat delayed in transfer to their independent writing, rather than immediate and concrete.

For same-ability pairs and for the less able members of all cross-ability pairs, particular attention should be paid to mechanisms for ensuring the generalization of gains accrued during collaborative writing to subsequent individual writing. While this may occur automatically with older writers, it cannot be taken for granted with younger writers.

Some sort of trouble-shooting facility needs to be available in case of problems, to which pairs can self-refer. Thus the Writer's Club might incorporate a writing clinic or surgery, at which pairs can seek the help of a wider cross-section of their peer group with a particular problem. This could also feature the presence of a professional at limited or alternating times.

Community-based projects may benefit from the use of a diary similar to those used in Paired Reading and Cued Spelling. Although the draft and best copy of the writing form a record in themselves, they will not tell the whole story of the process. The Self and Peer Evaluation Forms (see TRW website) offer another medium for feedback to the project organizer. These yield permanent written records as well as yet another purpose for writing.

As with the other paired methods, feedback meetings with participants to seek their views on the value of the method, possible improvements and alternative applications will be valuable.

In future cycles, diversification of formats could follow a successful first experience in one format (e.g. fixed role cross-ability PW peer tutoring followed by reciprocal role same-ability). Writers could become Helpers for other children in other contexts, or indeed Helpers could become Writers. Teachers may also wish to develop from an initial peer tutoring project to extension into parent tutoring at home (with the Writers already trained and experienced in the method and well placed to be at the center of quality assurance of the process in the home).

12 Does Paired Writing Work?

Recent conceptions of effective writing processes emphasize planning, ideas generation, text organization and meta-cognitive knowledge of the writing process. Writing is increasingly seen as a social rather than solitary activity. The importance of discussion, drafting and editing, a sense of audience, publishing, reader response, opportunities for peer assessment, and swift feedback mindfully received have been emphasized by many practitioners and researchers (e.g. Dyson, 1993, 1995).

Despite widespread acceptance of these in principle, concern has been expressed about the routine de-contextualized writing activities still found in some classrooms, and teacher over-emphasis on the superficial mechanics of writing (e.g. DeGroff, 1992). In the UK, although National Curriculum guidelines prescribed by central government include all the right elements, not all teachers are managing to deliver this in the classroom. Some still cling to traditional methods, which doubtless they feel have stood the test of time.

So how much promise does collaborative writing hold for developing more interactive and thoughtful writing processes?

Collaborative writing

Collaborative writing is not a single homogenous procedure, nor of itself necessarily a good thing. Saunders (1989) offered a typology of approaches to collaborative writing, including: co-writing (peers collaborate on every task), co-publishing (individuals produce a collaborative text based on individual texts), co-responding (individuals interact only during the revising process) and helping (writers voluntarily help one another during the writing process in an ad hoc manner). There are many different definitions of collaborative writing, so comparison of outcome studies must proceed with caution.

Outcome evaluations are in any event scarce. Much of the literature on collaborative writing is descriptive or ethnographic. Studies are difficult to compare or replicate, and are often vague about summative outcomes. Additionally, many of the existing outcome studies involved older writers in college or university, and the results cannot necessarily be generalized to younger age groups.

However, a few outcome studies have involved primary school children. Carr and Allen (1987) found that children as young as five could spontaneously elicit help from each other during the writing process, and that peers provided direct teaching when asked for help, irrespective of teacher prompting.

In Daiute's (1989) study of nine- to twelve-year-olds, children wrote stories collaboratively with a partner. Pairs engaged in discussion which was partly planned (organizing and controlled), and partly playful (exploring concepts and imagery, creating alliteration and inventing new or amusing words). The writing of the participants improved when there was a balance between planned and playful discussion. Daiute (1990) found boys used play more extensively than girls, successfully balancing play and control strategies, while girls tended to over-rely on control.

Daiute and Dalton (1993) studied fourteen low-achieving seven- to nine-year-old children, who used computers to write stories both individually and collaboratively. The effects of working in different types of pairs were considered: 'novice + expert' and 'true same-ability peers'. They proposed that same ability peer collaboration might be particularly important for 'exercising and increasing awareness of inert knowledge', while collaboration with an expert might be important for exposure to new knowledge, or for the refinement and organization of existing knowledge. This echoes the contrasting Piagetian and Vygotskian views of cooperative learning. In either case, repetition and co-construction appeared beneficial elements of the interactive process.

While collaborative writing may hold promise for developing more interactive and thoughtful writing processes, how can it be effectively scaffolded to support younger and less able students? Such students need to be fully engaged in the process, or the most able member of a collaborative group may do most of the work, fostering learned helplessness in the rest. The Paired Writing structure seeks to address these issues.

Common elements in Paired Writing

Obviously, the collaborative nature of Paired Writing is not at all novel. Cooperative writing groups of various sorts have been operated in elementary schools, high schools, colleges and universities for many years. Quite often this collaboration has occurred in larger groups than pairs, however. Also, this collaboration may have encompassed only a part of the writing process, rather than taking the whole piece through from start to finish, including evaluation.

Clearly, Paired Writing includes elements of process writing which have long been considered standard in developing better writers: Drafting, Editing, Best Copy. Beyond these, Step 1 merely offers a helping framework for the generation of ideas which is uncontroversial and capable of adaptation to individual need.

Perhaps peer assessment or evaluation (Step 6) will be found a little more unusual by some teachers, who may be concerned about the validity, reliability and possible social repercussions of this. Of course, peer assessment which is unilateral and does not specify any criteria for assessment is undesirable. But Paired Writing is not like that.

Pairs evaluate each other according to prescribed and familiar criteria, so motivation to be positive as well as analytical is maximized. Of course, peer assessment is also expected to have a reflexive impact on the next piece of writing done by the evaluators as well as the evaluated, an example of learning by assessment as well as learning by teaching.

The validity and reliability of the peer assessments can be expected to be as good as that of most teachers. Research has long since shown this to be so (O'Donnell and Topping, 1998). Teachers usually want to assess a few sample pieces of Paired Writing themselves for reassurance about the validity and reliability of peer assessment, however, especially with young or immature students to whom the idea is new.

Once the system is in full-swing, teachers should be freed of a huge burden of assessment and feedback. With Paired Writing, assessment and feedback are built into the process of generating the text. It is thus much swifter and more immediate, and therefore more effective.

Paired Writing also improves the self-evaluation skills of both pair members. These skills should then transfer to new situations, including those when either member of the pair is writing alone. This feature links with work on meta-cognition and self-instructional strategy training in writing.

Teachers may also find the low priority given to producing the best copy in Paired Writing somewhat unusual. Certainly written communication is useless unless it is legible to the intended audience. But the production of a best copy is essentially a mechanical act in Paired Writing. Tasks like these may shortly be taken over by technical devices such as voice recognition word processors. In Paired Writing, the important parts of creating new text are the thinking Steps 1, 2 and 4.

Where does Paired Writing fit?

Consideration of where Paired Writing fits involves consideration of where writing per se fits into school and everyday life. Writing has a number of purposes. Often these become confused. Writing may be used for creating, for communicating, for recording, or for assessment of thought processes, to name a few. Paired Writing lends itself well to creating, communicating and recording. It also promotes deeper thinking and understanding by requiring participants to structure their thoughts.

Very often writing has been used too much for assessment purposes – to check whether students have thought, understood, remembered. That is why some teachers are anxious trusting the grading of written assignments to peer evaluation. The use of writing as a form of outcome evaluation is actually very cumbersome and inefficient. Paired Writing makes evaluation an integral part of the learning process, without giving it excess emphasis, without burdening the teacher, and without turning children into surrogate teachers.

It is also common in schools for all children in a class to be expected to produce a piece of writing on a given subject. Paired Writing accommodates to this perfectly well, but can also easily be used in a situation where each pair chooses their own different topic.

If the whole class has to write on the same subject, the teacher will often choose to precede the Paired Writing with whole class or group discussion, brainstorming or other stimulation. Pairs can of course be paired to create conference groups of four. Some teachers like to heighten the writers' sense of purpose and audience by having some children (or pairs) read their composition to the whole class, perhaps from a specially designated author's chair.

Many teachers take great trouble to establish a sense of purpose and audience for writing in many other ways, for example writing stories, letters or buddy journals for children in other classes, other schools, other countries, or to parents, community personalities and agencies, or by producing information booklets, local or family histories, newsletters or newspapers. All of these are valuable components of a whole language or language experience approach to literacy. Paired Writing fits in well with all of them.

It is also worth remembering that just as Paired Reading can be done in any language and from bilingual texts, so Paired Writing may prove a powerful way of enabling children to express themselves in their language of greatest written proficiency while also learning to write in their second language.

In fact, just as with Paired Reading and Cued Spelling, the potential different applications for Paired Writing are numerous.

Controlled studies of Paired Writing

Three controlled studies of the effectiveness of Paired Writing in three different contexts in the UK were summarized in Topping *et al*. (2000). All the projects involved peer tutors.

Two of these projects used the Scottish National Curriculum Guidelines for assessment of writing products (Scottish Office Education Department, 1991). These specify attainment targets in writing (descriptive statements of minimum competency with chronological developmental expectations), at five broad developmental levels (A low to E high). Areas covered are: functional writing, personal writing, imaginative writing, punctuation and structure, spelling, handwriting and presentation, and knowledge about language, all broken down into smaller objectives. This was the prevailing national system, which was seen to have high face validity by the project schools. Inter-rater reliability using this system was found to be 80 per cent, considered adequate by the researchers.

The three action research projects reported below illustrate the effectiveness of Paired Writing in different contexts in ordinary elementary school classrooms. The Nixon project involved eleven-year-old tutors working with five-year-old emergent writers in two classes. The Sutherland project involved same-age tutoring in two classes of eight-year-olds (comparing fixed role cross-ability and reciprocal role same-ability tutoring). The Yarrow project involved same-age cross-ability tutoring within a behaviorally difficult class of ten-year-olds. In all control conditions, individual writers were monitored by and interacted with the teacher while writing, and were free to interact spontaneously with other individual writers if they wished.

The Nixon Project

In this project, the Paired Writing method was adapted for use in two parallel mixed-ability classrooms of five-year-old emergent writers, involving eleven-year-old cross-age peer tutors who were weak writers themselves. It was operated as part of a wider project aimed at promoting and encouraging emergent writing, which included establishing a writing stimulus play area with a home bay exemplifying the uses of literacy, and a writing resource area and author's chair. All 58 children in both classrooms experienced these wider developments, and from these, five were randomly selected from each class to participate in Paired Writing.

Some adaptation was made to the basic Paired Writing model, to enhance its appropriateness for young emergent writers. In Step 1 (Ideas Generation), the Helpers posed questions in the regular way, but responses were noted down by Writers in drawings as well as by Helpers in text. In Step 4 (Editing) the secondary emphasis concerning the mechanics of writing was omitted and the focus placed purely on meaning and order. Step 5 (Best Copy) was too onerous for these five-year-olds to accomplish by themselves.

For each emergent writer, three samples of individual writing for assessment were collected over a three-week period, before and after the project. Reliable assessment of emergent writing is difficult, since few of the existing scales are relevant to this level. A scale based on that of Gorman and Brooks (1996) was eventually adopted, and inter-rater reliability found to be 83 per cent. The mean pre-project individual writing scores were compared with post-project scores. All the children showed a statistically significant improvement, but the Paired Writers improved significantly more than those experiencing only the wider writing stimulus developments (see Nixon and Topping, 2000, for details).

During the project a very close relationship developed between the tutorial pairs. Both age groups enjoyed the experience, and other children clamored to become involved in Paired Writing. The sessions ran very smoothly, with the older tutors taking full responsibility for managing each session. The class teachers circulated freely to further support and coach individual pairs and to organize the activities of the rest of the children in the class. At the end of the project, all of the young tutees expressed enthusiasm for working with their older partner.

By the end of the project, nine out of ten of the tutors felt that their tutees were writing more independently, and offering more and better ideas for writing. All the tutors except one asserted that they liked doing Paired Writing, that it was easy to learn how to do, and that they enjoyed working with younger children. The class teachers of the tutors also noticed a difference, increased self-confidence being the most striking change.

The project clearly demonstrated the practical viability of an adapted version of Paired Writing with young emergent writers in a cross-age tutoring format.

The Sutherland Project

This study of eight-year-old children compared same-ability reciprocal role and cross-ability fixed role pairing. Two parallel mixed-ability classes of eight-year-olds in one school participated. One class contained the cross-ability experimental group and an individual writers control group. The other contained the same-ability experimental group and an individual writers control group.

Experimental and control children in both classes had two Paired Writing training sessions, and all retained the flowchart to consult while writing. The meta-cognitive content of the training was thus available to all. Individual writing completed immediately before and after the project was compared with each pair's Paired Writing completed during the project.

Comparing pre- and post-project individual writing, both groups of paired writers showed significant improvement relative to their controls, but this was more evident for the cross-ability pairs than the same-ability pairs (for full details, see Sutherland and Topping, 1999). On moving from individual to collaborative writing, the improvement in the cross-ability group largely represented improvement in the less able Writers. On returning to individual writing, the cross-ability group appeared to sustain the collaborative gains on average, but in fact this largely represented improvement in the more able Helpers. Thus there was some evidence that gains for the more able member of a cross-ability pair might not be evident in the short run – while actually writing collaboratively. Equally, on returning to individual writing, same-ability pairs might not generalize their collaborative gains readily to the individual writing environment, although in this project their overall pre–post performance was still significantly superior to their controls.

Participants did not report having any difficulty with the flow-chart, and Writers in particular said that its structure was helpful. The control participants, who had written individually throughout the project, indicated that they considered the Paired Writing flow-chart a useful tool in helping with the organization of their writing. Most of the participants reported feeling more confident about writing than they had prior to the beginning of the project.

The Yarrow Project

This project explored Paired Writing in same-age but cross-ability peer tutoring pairs. A problematic mixed-ability class of 28 ten-year-olds took part. Children were matched by gender and pre-test writing scores, divided into two equivalent groups, and groups assigned randomly to Paired Writing (Interaction) or Writing Individually (No Interaction) conditions. Both paired and individual writers received training (as in the Sutherland project), and were encouraged to use their personal copies of the flowchart throughout the project. This was adapted to separate Editing into two stages, the first dealing only with meaning and organization, to give these aspects priority before proceeding to consider spelling and punctuation. A Teacher Role card was also used to remind teachers supervising the class (especially when the regular teacher was absent) of the monitoring and coaching behavior required of them (see TRW website).

The meta-cognitive content of the Paired Writing training and flowchart, together with an increased rate of practice in writing during the project, led to improvements for all the children. However, Paired Writers showed significantly greater gains than children who wrote alone (i.e. the interactive component with the meta-cognitive component led to greater improvements than the latter alone). On the Writer Self-Perception Scale (Bottomley *et al.*, 1997), Paired Writers also showed more positive self-esteem as writers after the intervention than those who had written alone.

Paired Writing tutors and tutees both showed gains. Without the continuing support of their Helpers, the interactive Writers' quality of writing tended to decrease on return to individual writing, but was still significantly higher than at pre-test. The Helpers, who had shown a lesser improvement during the intervention, showed generalization of what they had learned from their tutoring role in their own improved post-test scores (see Yarrow and Topping, 2001, for details).

The class teacher and children in this study were not experienced in a process approach to writing, and a number of the children had behavioral difficulties. Nevertheless, the Paired Writing structure facilitated the adoption of a process approach, with no specific teaching beyond the two sessions of Paired Writing training.

Conclusion

Paired Writing appears to be a flexible, robust, and effective system in peer tutoring applications which can have beneficial effects on both tutors and tutees even in adverse circumstances. Controlled studies are needed of PW with parent and volunteer tutors.

13 How To Evaluate Paired Writing

The discussion of research designs and methods for Paired Reading applies here also (reading Chapter 5 before this chapter will be very helpful). Measures will of course be different.

As with all evaluation, this should be conducted with reference to the objectives set for the project, which may be academic, affective, social, or a combination of these.

Is Paired Writing to be targeted on many types of writing for many purposes, or just one? Located within Language Arts or English lessons, or operated across the curriculum, or the first leading into the second? In any event, there is clearly a need to check if it meets the primary objective – the production of better quality writing than would occur if writers worked separately. But what of generalization to subsequent individual writing? Are gains for both tutors and tutees targeted, and how will this be reflected in strategic organization of the project? Might some of the wider meta-cognitive gains be delayed, making follow-up important if the impact of the project is not to be underestimated?

Problems of measurement

In considering the production of better quality writing, the word 'quality' is important. Paired Writing is not concerned with yielding a greater volume of writing, since this of itself is worthless, as is reading fast without understanding.

However, measurement of quality of writing is problematic. This can be approached by assessing written output against some widely accepted criteria generally considered indicative of good writing. This is what teachers informally do all the time when marking a piece of writing.

Even when a clearly articulated set of criteria of quality is established, questions remain. Are the criteria actually widely accepted? Are they based on empirical research? Are they unambiguous and capable of yielding high inter-rater reliabilities? How objective can the assessment of the content of creative writing ever be?

Possible elements for inclusion in a criterion-referenced assessment and evaluation strategy of the quality indicator type are considered in more detail below. This common framework could be applied to many different types of writing, completed for many different purposes and audiences, in many different settings.

However, there is an alternative approach to the assessment and evaluation of writing, which we may call the objectives approach. Any piece of writing can be assumed to have a purpose. The purposes or objectives of a piece of writing are certainly set by its composer. However, additional and/or different objectives may also be set by the recipient of the writing, and possibly by a third party with some vested interest in the outcome (e.g. a teacher).

Disagreements about the worth of a piece of writing often stem from the different views of different involved parties about the objectives of the exercise. Frequently these differing views are not clearly articulated, so writers are never clear what they have to do to be right. Quite often not even the audience, client or customer for the piece are specified. If the objectives of a piece of writing are discussed, negotiated and agreed at the outset, a much higher quality written product can be expected.

Clearly, if the objectives of the piece of writing are specified in this way, the writing can subsequently be evaluated with reference to these objectives. This does not, of course, remove all the subjectivity in the assessment process, but it may reduce it.

However, the objectives approach to assessing writing presents difficulties from a research point of view. The objectives set for a piece of writing will reflect the idiosyncratic needs and objectives specified by the interested parties in that situation at that time. Objectives will probably be different in different situations. Evaluation by objectives yields multiple individual outcomes which are varied and difficult to summarize or aggregate. Consequently the overall general picture is hard to see, and comparisons difficult to make.

A problem with the traditional assessment of writing has been that some teachers mixed the quality indicator method with the objectives method without realizing it. As a result, neither teacher nor child were clear enough about how the assessment was carried out, and some of the beneficial learning effects of precise feedback from the assessment process were lost.

In the next section, the focus will be on the criterion-referenced quality indicator method. Those wishing to supplement this with individualized objectives-based assessment will be able to use their own initiative to do so.

Criterion-referenced assessment

Frameworks for this type of assessment have been proposed by several workers in the field. Some of these will be reviewed below. Many common elements will be evident. The elements you may actually use in your own project will vary in response to different situations. A relevant selection could be made from this item bank of generally accepted indicators.

An early and widely known quality indicator was the Analytic Scale of Diederich (1974). This is composed of eight separate categories, each scored on a five-point scale by the assessor. Categories referring to matters of content were given double weighted scores to reflect their importance in relation to matters of form. The categories were: ideas, organization, wording, usage, punctuation, spelling, handwriting – and 'flavor'.

Cooper (1977) later promulgated a similar scale for holistic evaluation of writing, but its reliability was low. Karegianes *et al.* (1980) used a modified version of the Analytic Scale (omitting flavor) and found adequate inter-rater reliability (coefficients of 0.87 at pre-test and 0.85 at post-test) between two experienced English teachers when assessing essays all of which were on the same topic. Comparing the quality of two pieces of writing that are on different topics is much more tricky, of course.

Carlson and Roellich (1983) developed an eleven-item scale named the Indicator for Rating Performance, Grades 6–12. This was intended to be used by children during peer assessment. Differing numbers of points can be awarded by raters in each category: Purpose (10), Information (20), Organization (15), Variety and Precision of Language (10), Grammatical Completeness, Clarity and Variety (15), Usage (5), Capitalization (5), Punctuation (5), Spelling (10), Legibility and Presentation (5), Originality and Creativity (10). Complex definitions and simple Evaluation Score Sheets are provided. There is no evidence of reliability nor any information about the basis of the differential points system.

Isaacson (1988) considered the five most important assessment dimensions for writing to be fluency, content, conventions, syntax and vocabulary. He noted that those assessment categories which are concerned with the superficial characteristics of a piece of writing are usually those with highest reliability, and the inclusion of many such categories in a total scale artificially inflates its apparent reliability.

Fluency can be defined as the number of words written (presumably in any given time); Content as originality of ideas, organization of thought, coherence, awareness of audience and maturity of style; Conventions as spelling, margins, punctuation, handwriting, capitalization, micro-grammar (e.g. word endings); Syntax as macro-grammar – length and complexity of sentences; and Vocabulary as originality and maturity in choice of words (relative to own previous performance).

Although Isaacson (1988) refers to much background research, no evidence is given from field trials of his conclusions. This is also true of the error analysis system described by Goodman *et al.* (1987), which was preoccupied with deficits rather than competencies.

Contributions from a behavioral perspective came from Hopman and Glynn (1988, 1989). They reviewed research demonstrating that many aspects of writing behavior can be improved simply by specifying the required behavior and positively reinforcing it. Aspects which have been improved in this way include handwriting speed and legibility, capitalization, punctuation, and use of prepositional phrases and other parts of speech. Correspondence training (self-verbalization before action) has also produced good results (e.g. Hopman and Glynn, 1989).

Nor have these positive effects been confined to aspects of form and mechanics in writing which have preoccupied teachers for centuries. A number of studies (e.g. Glover and Gary, 1976; Harrop and McCann, 1984) have shown improvements in fluency (defined as the number of different written productions), flexibility (number of verb forms), and number of words per production and originality, supported by gains on tests of creative thinking.

Graham and Harris (1989) have made a number of contributions to this field. They note that learning disabled children often have a production problem rather than the wider information processing problem which may be all too readily assumed. Thus, MacArthur and Graham (1987) found that learning disabled children's dictated compositions were three to four times longer than their hand-written or word-processed papers. The written compositions of learning disabled children are characterized by the omission of critical structural content elements (e.g. how the story ends) and the inclusion of much irrelevant or nonfunctional information. Pre-writing planning, a sense of audience and overall cohesiveness is often lacking. Accordingly, Graham and Harris (1989) sought to train such children in self-instructional strategic prompting procedures (somewhat similar to correspondence training).

Changes in writing performance were analysed through measures of functional elements (premise, reasons, conclusions, elaborations) and nonfunctional elements, number of words written and cohesiveness. Scoring procedures for these were largely based on those developed previously by Scardamalia *et al.* (1982). Reliability coefficients were: total number of elements 0.89, premise 0.77, reasons 0.79, conclusions 1.00, elaborations 0.83, nonfunctional 0.97, coherence 0.83 and number of words 0.99. These are certainly adequately high, but replication at these levels from other sites would be welcome.

Additionally, pre-writing time was recorded. A scale developed by Graham and Harris for assessing the schematic structure of stories was also applied. This scored eight story elements: main character, locale, time, starter event, goal, action, ending and reaction. (Of course, this scale would be of little utility with non-fiction writing.) Generalization to a new setting and maintenance of improvements over time were also assessed. The self-image of the participants as writers was investigated on a before and after basis.

Common elements

Considering all the analytical categories which have been proposed in the literature, one might expect to find greater agreement on the more readily measurable aspects of form and convention than on those of creativity, originality and communicative content. This is indeed the case, although there is also a good deal of agreement on issues of content.

Common elements in the item bank of quality indicators can be divided into those referring to content and those referring to form.

Content
1. Purpose and Awareness of Audience
2. Originality and Creativity of Ideas
3. Organization and Coherence of Structure
4. Variety and Precision of Wording

Form
5. Legibility of Handwriting
6. Speed and Volume of Production
7. Grammar
8. Spelling
9. Punctuation
10. Capitalization

If the temptation to use this apparently tidy ten-point scale is overwhelming, remember the relative importance of content and form. You may wish to double score the content items to counterbalance this (cf. Diederich, 1974).

Also remember that some of these aspects are not considered particularly relevant in Paired Writing (e.g. legibility), or are taken as read. Paired Writing should not be expected necessarily to result in improvements in these aspects.

Be under no illusions that this scale is magically scientific although it is based on more evidence than what most teachers traditionally do. Nevertheless, it is capable of generating worthless results if used in too casual a manner. Ideally, carry out your own local reliability check on a small sample of scripts which are rated by yourself and a colleague without knowledge of their originators. Only when you have reached at least 75 per cent agreement can you begin to feel your results are reasonably reliable.

Even with a relatively reliable scale, the major problem with the assessment of writing is the enormous amount of time involved. The only redeeming feature is that probably you would have had to grade those scripts anyhow, albeit in less detail.

Recent developments

Similar scales continue to be developed. The work of Bratcher is very useful to elementary school teachers, not least because her books include extensive examples of children's writing (e.g. Bratcher, 1994). In the UK, Gorman and Brooks (1996) have produced a scale particularly useful in relation to the problematic issue of the assessment of young children's writing.

On the TRW website, a very simple scale designed for teacher use with very young emergent writers will be found, the Emergent Writing Evaluation Questionnaire for teachers.

Where national or other wide-ranging curriculum guidelines on the teaching of writing are in place, these are often accompanied by prescribed scales for the assessment of writing (as is the case in England and Scotland, although the scales are not the same) (e.g. Scottish Office Education Department, 1991). However, these scales are no more likely to be psychometrically stable or empirically based than others mentioned above. They merely have superficial face validity in their native territory.

Professional organizations also promote the development of criterion-referenced assessment scales and other measurement tools. In the US, the National Council of Teachers of English (NCTE) (www.ncte.org) has been active in this regard, and a visit to their website to check out their latest efforts is recommended.

Norm-referenced tests

Teachers may have doubts about whether a norm-referenced (standardized) test can provide valid and reliable measures of writing ability. However, such instruments do exist.

Lagana (1972) used the STEP Writing Test and STEP Essay Test as pre-test and post-test measures with experimental and control groups in a writing experiment involving both individualized learning and peer group learning. On both tests the experimental group performed significantly better at post-test than the control group who had received traditional composition instruction. Experimental subjects made particular gains in the categories of organization, critical thinking and appropriateness. The test results were supplemented with more subjective data.

The Test of Written Language (Hammill and Larsen, 1983) is another example of this genre. This covers five elements of written expression: mechanics of handwriting, meaningful content, convention conformity (spelling, capitalization, punctuation), syntactical structure and creative (or cognitive) component. An over-emphasis on mechanics and form is evident, despite evidence of very low correlation between grammatical knowledge and quality of written output (Kuykendall, 1975).

Separate standardized tests of restricted aspects of the writing process such as spelling, punctuation, capitalization and understanding of vocabulary can also be found. In the UK, the Bristol Achievement Tests (Brimer, 1969) go a little further and include sub-tests of paragraph meaning, sentence organization and organization of ideas. How these sub-skill tests relate to the total organic writing process is another question. How they address issues of purpose, audience and motivation is problematic. There are many fewer standardized tests of writing than of reading, and in many countries there are no standardized tests available. Where standardized tests of writing are available, they vary greatly from country to country. Virtually none of the tests used in the UK are used in the US, and vice versa. Also, such tests can go out of date quickly.

Consequently, those wishing to use such tests would do better to scrutinize the catalogs of the major educational test suppliers in their country (most of which are now available on-line) or access more general compendiums of tests, such as the Buros database of mental measurements (also now available on-line). The latter reports on freely available public domain tests as well as commercially available tests.

Self-concept and attitude

Given that tests of self-concept and attitude to reading are rare, and tend not to be very stable, it is unsurprising that such assessments relating to writing are very scarce indeed. One notable exception is the Writer Self-Perception Scale of Bottomley *et al.* (1997).

Subjective feedback

As with the other paired methods, verbal feedback can be solicited from participants in a variety of settings, but is often difficult to summarize (see Chapter 5).

A simple questionnaire for gathering subjective feedback from tutees and peer or parent tutors will be found on the TRW website. There also are brief interview schedules for peer tutors, for peer tutees, and for teachers monitoring peer tutor PW projects. These are intended for use with individuals, but could also help structure feedback discussions with groups. It is often helpful if participants see the key questions before coming to feedback sessions.

Part Four
Cued Spelling

14 What Is Cued Spelling?

Spelling is a curriculum area which is both neglected and controversial. Few teachers seem to enjoy teaching spelling and fewer children enjoy learning it. The range of strategies, materials and methods is probably smaller and less varied than in any other basic skills area. Yet government and employers continue to assert the importance of spelling. While spelling might not be as important as reading or the creative aspects of writing, it is still important.

Cued Spelling is to spelling what Paired Reading is to reading. So why isn't it called Paired Spelling? Because so many different activities have been subsumed under the label of Paired Reading, a more specific name to indicate a specific procedure was thought necessary. Paired Spelling may or may not be Cued Spelling as described below.

Cued Spelling is deliberately designed to incorporate many of the positive features of Paired Reading. It is a simple and enjoyable technique for one-to-one tutoring by non-professionals on a brief but regular basis. It raises confidence and motivation without needing any special materials or expensive equipment. It is used for parent tutoring, peer tutoring and for adult learners with spelling problems.

It also incorporates many of the features of other tried and tested approaches to teaching spelling. It then combines these in a package which is easily and widely used.

Cued Spelling is usually done three times a week for an initial 'trial' period of six weeks. Each session takes about fifteen minutes.

At the outset, Cued Spelling looks rather complicated. Don't be put off. You can train seven-year-olds to do it in half an hour – it is a lot simpler than it looks.

The basic structure of the technique comprises the Ten Steps, the Four Points to Remember and two Reviews. The structure is illustrated in the Cued Spelling Flowchart, available on the TRW website. You may wish to print a copy of this now, to refer to while you read the rest of this chapter.

The Ten Steps and Four Points apply to every individual target word worked upon by the pair. The Speed Review covers all target words for a particular session and the Mastery Review covers all the target words for one week or a longer period if desired.

The Ten Steps

1. The tutee chooses high interest target words irrespective of complexity. These may be drawn from (or collected in) any curriculum area in the school week, or from outside interests.

2. The pair check the spelling of the word in a dictionary or elsewhere and put a master version in their Cued Spelling Diary. (The CS Diary is available on the TRW website). They usually also add the word to the top of a piece of paper on which subsequent attempts will be made.

3. The pair then read the word out loud together (Paired Reading style), then the tutee reads the word aloud alone. This ensures that the tutee is capable of accurate reading and articulation of the word. Without this, spelling attempts are unlikely to succeed!

4. The tutee then chooses cues (prompts or reminders) to enable him or her to remember the written structure of the word. These cues may be phonic sounds, letter names, syllables or other fragments or 'chunks' of words, or wholly idiosyncratic mnemonic devices. Tutees are encouraged to consider and choose cues which fit with their own cognitive structures, that make sense and are memorable to them. Although a tutor may make suggestions, the decision on cueing rests wholly with the tutee. The Mnemonic Strategies and Mnemonic Ideas handouts on the TRW website give tutors and tutees further help with cues.

5. Once cues are decided on, the pair say the cues out loud together.

6. The tutee then says the cues out loud while the tutor

writes the word down on scrap paper to this 'dictation'. The tutee is provided with a demonstration or model of the required behavior.

7. The tutor says the cues out loud while the tutee writes the word down.
8. The tutee then says the cues and writes the word at the same time.
9. The tutee writes the word as quickly as possible. The tutee may or may not decide to recite the cues out loud or may well recite them sub-vocally.
10. The tutee again reads the word out loud as a reminder of the wholeness of the target word and its associated meaning.

The Four Points

The Four Points cover aspects of the technique relevant to its practical application.

1. At every attempt at writing a target word, the tutor or the tutee ensures that previous attempts are covered up to avoid copying.
2. Every time there is a written attempt on a target word, the tutee checks the attempt. The tutor only intervenes if the tutee proves unable to check the attempt accurately.
3. If tutees have written a word incorrectly, they are encouraged to cross it out vigorously to help its deletion from their memory. At an incorrect attempt, the correction procedure is merely that the pair return to the Step preceding the one at which the error was made.
4. Tutors praise tutees regularly for good performance. In particular, tutors praise for:
   - tutees correcting their mistakes before checking with the master version
   - getting each word right at Step 9
   - getting words right at Reviews (see below).

More details of the nature of praise and the criteria for its application are given in training meetings.

The Two Reviews

There is a Speed Review at the end of each tutoring session. The tutee writes all the target words for that session as quickly as possible from dictation in random order. The tutee then self-checks all the words with the master version in the Cued Spelling Diary.

Target words which are incorrect at speed review have the Ten Steps applied again, perhaps with the choice of different Cues. In practice, tutees make only a small proportion of errors at speed review. The requirement to re-apply the Ten Steps is not as onerous as it sounds.

At the end of each week, a Mastery Review is conducted. The tutee writes all the target words for the whole week as quickly as possible in random order from dictation. The tutee then self-checks all the words with the master version in the Cued Spelling Diary.

No specific error correction method is prescribed for Mastery Review. It is left to the pair to negotiate what they want to do about errors. Many pairs choose to include failed words in the next week's target words.

A reproducible handout for tutors and tutees (CS How To Do It) will be found on the TRW website. This describes the whole CS method in more detail than the flowchart, but more simply than the description above. You may want to look at it now. This handout should be distributed at the end of a training meeting for future reference.

How does Cued Spelling work?

Cued Spelling contains little that is new. It incorporates well-known methods and aspects of accepted good practice. The assembly is as important as the components. It was designed as a coherent package, structured and flexible at the same time.

Just like Paired Reading with reading, Cued Spelling does not assume that the tutee possesses any particular spelling 'sub-skills'. CS is designed to promote the most effective use of whatever skills the tutee does possess. Like Paired Reading, it offers 'positive practice'.

The technique has been designed and structured to be highly interactive, but in operation it is democratic (mutually self-governing) rather than autocratic. It is intended to provide a supportive framework to scaffold self-managed learning.

There is evidence that spellers use a variety of strategies in a highly idiosyncratic manner, so any requirement to use a specific mnemonic strategy is likely to merely further inhibit an already poor speller. There is also evidence that when children select their own spelling words, they tend to choose more difficult words, but are as successful as with easier words chosen by adults.

Work on mnemonic strategies has emphasized the importance of meaningfulness to the tutee. Thus the Cued Spelling technique fits in well with recent trends towards individualized and self-governed learning of spelling skills.

The technique is 'failure-free' – it eliminates anxiety and promotes self-confidence. Swift error correction and support procedures are built in. The technique is also flexible, useful across a wide range of age and ability, with word lists of variety and complexity.

Tutees are encouraged to select interesting and motivating individualized material; some both want and need to master quite specialized vocabulary. Additionally, tutees largely control the procedure, deciding themselves on the degree of support they require at any moment.

Modeling gives tutees an example of correct performance which they can copy. Being left to work everything out on your own often results in a high error rate, over-frequent correction and faulty learning.

Praise is essential to reinforce correct responses but also to promote tutor behavior incompatible with damaging criticism. The strong emphasis on understanding is essential for the task to be purposeful for the tutee.

The technique promotes fluency, eliminating stopping and starting and pondering at length about particular words. The steps represent small incremental stages. A pair should be able to work through the steps very quickly on easy words, but it should not become boring and frustrating on difficult words.

Tutees have individual attention and immediate feedback from their tutors. With improved support, motivation and concentration, tutees work on a larger number of words than in more traditional approaches, increasing the amount of practice.

The nature of the activity should ensure a high level of time on task.

There is a wide gulf between learning to write a word accurately during rote learning or a tutoring session and being able to write it at a different time in a totally different context (for example during creative free writing). The emphasis in the later stages of the technique on speeded performance is drawn from the concept of 'fluency' in Precision Teaching. This aspect is included to promote generalization over time and contexts, since otherwise there is a danger that the tutee will merely have learned spelling tricks, while continuing to spell words incorrectly.

Lastly, and perhaps most importantly, the technique is clear, straightforward and enjoyable. Both tutor and tutee are easily trained in its use. Neither one of the pair becomes confused, anxious or bad-tempered about their spelling work together.

You may wish to summarize these advantages in a handout for potential participants in a project.

Many of these advantages are in line with research on self-efficacy and motivated learning. Regularity and frequency of success is as important as the amount of success. Tutees with difficulties may attribute failure to their own inadequacy rather than to deficiencies in teaching. Tutees need to see that success is the result of their own efforts rather than an excess of support or random chance.

Verbalization by the tutee has been shown to facilitate strategic encoding and retention in learning and to promote systematic working. Regularity, frequency and immediacy of feedback are particularly important when tutees are faced with very complex tasks or are handicapped by learning disabilities.

Naturally, the method is not intended just to help tutees remember lists of words. As tutees create their own cues they must think about the auditory, visual, syntactic and semantic structure of the word. It may well be that it is this self-directed interaction rather than the cue itself which improves retention. With experience and by making connections with taught spelling knowledge, tutees more readily perceive consistencies in word structures.

Cued Spelling provides a framework within which the tutee can 'make sense of spelling' – but make their own sense of it. Spelling is conceptual as well as perceptual, and tutees need to form predictive concepts about how words work. As the interactive procedures of Cued Spelling involve them in comparing and contrasting, they may organize and integrate these concepts for themselves more effectively.

Teachers sometimes have worries about the Cued Spelling method before trying it out. They may wonder if the method promotes 'mere memorization' or supports spelling exclusively by 'cues'. In practice, the tutees remember the words but not usually the cues. As they become more used to the method, their cues become more systematic and reflective of the regularities in our language as well as their own favored learning style. Their powers of prediction of regularities in new words certainly increase. The evaluation results showing generalization of improved spelling capability to the completely new words in norm-referenced spelling tests are a clear indication of that.

How does Cued Spelling relate to other methods?

There is less than full agreement about how specific spelling instruction should be integrated within the curriculum. Is good spelling caught or does it have to be taught? From a visual orientation, work on word patterns and word clusters is often popular, but the skills may not be retained and generalized to free writing. Other teachers favor phonic strategies, yet less than half of the words in the English language are phonically regular. With older children, spelling rules come more into play – but the complexity of our language means a vast number of rules and exceptions need to be remembered and applied.

Many teachers will be familiar with the Look-Cover-Write-Check methods. This has the advantage of being quick, cheap and self-managed by children. Unfortunately the method also has the disadvantage of being primarily visually oriented. By itself, it may be suitable and effective for some words and some children. But only some. Thus you will find elements of Look-Cover-Write-Check within the Cued Spelling package, but CS goes further, offers more options and individual flexibility, and is effective with many more words and many more children.

Just as with learning to read, there are many different pathways to becoming a competent speller. There may be developmental differences as well as individual differences. There is some evidence that younger children tend to rely on auditory information irrespective of the nature of the word, while for older children visual information

produces better results. As with reading, over-teaching in any specific narrow instructional channel can do more harm than good, particularly where the type of instruction does not correspond to the
tutee's strongest sensory modality and/or learning style. Teachers still
sometimes try to teach all children to spell in the way they themselves learned to spell successfully. But of course this is not the best
way for all (or perhaps even many) of the children. However, most
teachers have no time to analyse the individual spelling profile of
every child in the class and prescribe and manage a wide range of
individual spelling programs.

One solution is to help children to manage their own learning. As
one of the strands in a spelling instruction program, teachers can
adopt methods which free the children to follow their own favored
pathways, but within a strongly supportive general framework. With
Cued Spelling, this can be done in an interactive way which involves
the children in evaluating for themselves the success of their own
strategies. However, as with Paired Reading, Cued Spelling is not
intended to constitute the whole of the spelling curriculum in
school. Cued Spelling is different from, but complementary to, regular teacher-directed classroom instruction.

Cued Spelling is not intended to replace other methods. Computer aided learning, tactile and kinesthetic methods, and special
phonic dictionaries can happily be used in conjunction with Cued
Spelling, or as a periodic alternative to provide variety and promote
generalization.

Adaptations

Cued Spelling as described above has been used successfully with
tutees as young as seven. More able and mature under-sevens may
be able to use the technique. However, adaptation for use with
younger and less able children may be indicated. A suggested abbreviated Cued Spelling procedure for this purpose will be found on
the TRW website. Remember that it has yet to be evaluated like the
full CS procedure.

15 How To Organize Cued Spelling

Cued Spelling projects follow many of the organizational guidelines for Paired Reading projects (reading Chapter 3 before this chapter is very helpful). You will be able to use much of the PR parent and peer tutoring Planning Proformas (see TRW website). The context and objectives sections apply. Similar organizational questions must be answered about recruitment, selection and matching, training, organization of contact, support and monitoring, feedback, and evaluation. One planning area which is very different is materials. In what follows, repetition will be avoided as far as possible, emphasis being given to significant organizational differences for CS as compared to PR.

Context, objectives and recruitment should be considered and specified much as for Paired Reading.

Selection and matching

Potential Cued Spellers should be able to read well enough to interpret the CS flowchart with practice, know the names and sounds of some letters, and be able to write in a way which is legible to their partner. Those who cannot write might still be able to do Cued Spelling by using a typewriter or computer, letter cards or plastic letters.

As with Paired Reading, you need to consider how many children you can effectively support and monitor at one time. You may wish to start with a few volunteers. The others can do other kinds of spelling work, and give you interesting possibilities for evaluative comparison. As with PR, you do need a group of sufficient size and variety to offer mutual support and not feel stigmatized or singled out.

Tutors do not necessarily have to be better spellers than tutees. If they are about as good (or bad) as each other, they need to take special care to look up every word carefully in the dictionary. They also need to be very careful to copy the master version into Cued Spelling Diaries accurately. Otherwise there is a great danger of the pair learning incorrect spellings. Cued Spelling is a powerful procedure – if you don't start off right, you will spell the word wrong thereafter.

This possibility of same-ability pairing opens up interesting possibilities. A parent who is of limited spelling ability could work with a child of similar ability, or sibling tutoring could operate between children of similar or different ages. Particularly in peer tutoring, you may wish to opt for reciprocal tutoring. The tutor and tutee could swap roles at predetermined intervals, by session or by week.

There are many advantages to reciprocal tutoring. Everybody gets to be a tutor during the project, so nobody feels inferior. Everybody knows the role of both tutor and tutee, so re-matching pairs when covering for absences is much easier. The variety helps stave off boredom.

Of course, both members of the pair end up learning their own and their partner's words. This could be tested by having the tutees give terminal total Mastery Reviews on the tutee's words to the tutors, rather than the other way round.

For peer tutoring matching purposes, draw up a ranked list of more to less able spellers compiled from spelling test results or class observation. If you opt for cross-ability fixed role tutoring, draw a line through the middle of the list to separate tutors from tutees. Then match the most able tutor to the most able tutee, and so on down the list to maintain roughly the same differential in spelling ability in each pair.

However, if you opt for same-ability (and probably reciprocal role) tutoring, do not divide the ranked list. Just match first with second, third with fourth, and so on. You will see that one disadvantage of same-ability tutoring is that the two weakest spellers in the class will be working together. This is acceptable so long as they are not also the most disorganized and distractible. You will need to monitor them closely in any case.

As with PR, do not worry unduly about boy/girl pairs, but do not pair obviously non-compatible children. Consider appointing spare tutors.

Materials

Participant pairs need a pen or pencil, scrap paper, a piece of card, an appropriate dictionary, a CS Flowchart, a CS Diary and a CS collecting book. The flowchart and diary are easily reproduced (see TRW website). The collecting book is just a small notebook with blank pages. Little time or cost is involved.

Providing dictionaries can be more difficult. Some schools do not have enough for each pair to have their own. Some families will not have one at home and a loan from school may have to be explored. The type of dictionary is also an issue. In a regular mixed-ability class there is usually only one standard dictionary issued. This will be too hard for the weaker pairs to access and will not contain the difficult words the more able pairs wish to work on. A range of dictionaries is needed.

Remember that for Cued Spelling it is assumed that the tutees know the meaning of the words they choose. Definitional dictionaries are not needed for this purpose. Schools may wish to invest in a number of small spelling dictionaries. These are cheap because they do not give definitions. They usually include plurals and declensions with which spellers have trouble.

Training

Training tutors and tutees together is usual and the least time-consuming. (However, some schools have trained children first and then parents later.) Ensure that trainees have pen or pencil, scrap paper, piece of card, appropriate dictionary and sample page from spelling diary. The tutees must have collected five words they want to learn how to spell correctly.

Be welcoming. Establishing an informal, friendly, communicating atmosphere is essential. Briefly describe national and local CS projects and mention positive evaluation results. Highlight the differences between Cued Spelling and more traditional approaches:

- use of high interest, specialist, hard words
- use of any friendly tutor
- brief but regular and frequent commitment.

Emphasize that it may be fun but it will still be real work.

Distribute the Ten Steps or the abbreviated procedure flowcharts, one per pair, at the start of the meeting. Explain that Cued Spelling has 10 Steps, 4 Points to Remember and 2 Reviews. Emphasise that although it seems complicated, it is not difficult. You may wish to give a quick demonstration of a pair going through the Ten Steps on a word (taking little over two minutes), to reinforce this.

Then talk about the Ten Steps. Refer to the CS flowchart all the time. You may wish to display the flowchart on an overhead projector. Demonstrate the steps yourself or show the CS video (see the TRW website for details). A live demonstration of CS often lacks clarity of small detail and tends to be less successful. A fast demonstration followed by a slow one with pauses for commentary are most effective.

When you come to Step 4 Choosing Cues, elaborate on what this means. Mention the alphabetic, phonic, syllabic and mnemonic options. Give an example of each. You will need to use a chalkboard or write on overhead transparencies to show what you mean. Solicit examples of 'hard words to spell' from the tutees. Solicit suggestions from the group for different cues for these. Strongly emphasize that different people will use different cues. There is no such thing as the 'right' cue, only the cue which is best (most effective) for the individual. However, with peer tutoring you may wish to relate cueing to recent classroom instruction in spelling.

Follow a similar procedure with the Four Points and the Two Reviews.

Then have the pairs go off to practice. They will need tables and chairs for this. Access to the required materials should be indicated. You might wish to display suggested 'practice' words for those who have arrived without their own. Likewise, arrange substitute tutees/ tutors or role play if some 'pairs' are incomplete.

Experienced Cued Spellers should then circulate and check practice. There should be a monitor/trainee ratio sufficient to ensure a minimum of three minutes individual attention for each pair during practice. As with PR, use a three-step remediation sequence for those needing further coaching:

1. Praise good practice and point out faulty aspects, giving further verbal advice.

2. Join in with pair and proceed as a triad.
3. Take over from the tutor and re-demonstrate with the tutee.

On return to the large group, the trainer can comment generally on practice observed and solicit questions. Then brief the group about organizational issues:

- time commitment
- where to collect words from
- where to keep collected words (CS collecting book)
- how to keep records in the CS Diary
- when and how to have records verified and responded to by the teacher.

Tutees should show their CS Diaries to the teacher once each week.

Emphasize that the children are encouraged to choose words from their school spelling books, graded free writing, relevant project work, special Cued Spelling displays of common problem words, or groups of words selected by the teacher as developmentally appropriate. Tutees should collect these in a CS collecting book, so they always have a pool of suitable words ready.

Distribute the additional materials required: CS Diary with sufficient pages for the initial project period, CS collecting books, CS Mnemonic Strategies and Mnemonic Ideas handouts (see TRW website).

In CS Diaries, each page includes space to write the master list of up to ten words on every day of the week, together with boxes to record daily Speed Review and weekly Mastery Review scores and spaces for comments from tutor (daily) and teacher (weekly).

Describe the monitoring, support, trouble-shooting and feedback arrangements, much as with PR.

Specify the initial contract – a minimum of five words per day for three days per week (time about fifteen minutes per session) for six weeks. Secure verbal or written commitment from the participants. Participating children might receive a badge.

Allow one hour fifteen minutes for the meeting, with additional time for refreshment and general discussion.

Contact

Organization of contact is much the same as for peer tutored Paired Reading. Try to keep the three sessions per week well spaced to counteract boredom. Schedule fifteen minutes per session and expect five words and Review to be completed in this time. If pairs choose to go on longer in their own time, they can proceed at a more leisurely pace.

Remember chairs and tables will be needed and some noise will result. The demands on space will be significant. Children like to spread over into other spaces for extra privacy.

Support and monitoring

The advice for PR in Chapter 3 (p. 33) applies in CS. In a peer tutoring project you will find the children readily ask for help with difficult words. Make sure you give them only correct spellings – many teachers are more sure about their own spelling capabilities than they have cause to be! Encourage checking with the dictionary.

As you observe pairs in action, check that there are four correct written attempts for every word. If you cannot see at least four attempts, the pair are missing out some Steps.

Check the pair's organization of the necessary materials. Too much clutter on the table can result in much fussing and time spent off task. Ensure that mistakes are corrected as the method prescribes and generosity (or slackness) does not creep in. Some tutors are too helpful and do too much for their tutee, risking creating dependence and learned helplessness. Emphasize that tutoring does not equate to doing something for the tutee. Encourage an emphasis on speed and high rates of time on task. Keep an eye out for social friction.

Vet any creative adaptations a pair start making to the method very carefully for effectiveness and mutual acceptability.

Keep a close watch on the words chosen. Some tutees may choose words they already know, while others may choose extremely difficult words of very doubtful long-term utility. Neither will do much to help the development of generalized understanding about the structure of words. A simple initial rule is 'three for school use and two just for fun'.

Watch out for pairs who have locked into narrow themes (for example football) and are focussing exclusively on a specialist vocabulary. The children may need reminding that the point of CS is to help them spell better in the course of everyday free writing. Being able to perform a few exotic but otherwise useless spelling tricks is not the goal. Also beware of pairs who like to create baroque mnemonics as an art form, irrespective of any value in improving spelling.

Tutees tend to express two main difficulties – finding words and finding cues. Promoting the collection of words is important. Should the (cautious) teacher have chosen to set a ceiling of difficulty on words chosen, the most competent pairs may soon feel they can spell everything below that ceiling and frustration can set in.

All pairs will have difficulty finding interesting cues for some words. Occasional whole-class sessions on cueing can be held to brainstorm good cues for such words, elaborating different approaches (see Mnemonic Strategies and Mnemonic Ideas handouts on TRW website) and linking cueing to regular spelling instruction. Encourage comparing and contrasting to help children perceive, relate and map spelling regularities. Set up a display board for favorite mnemonics.

Partners can be exchanged at a later stage to increase novelty and widen the social effects of the tutoring.

Remember Cued Spelling makes you more of a teacher – a coordinator of effective learning experiences in and out of school. The organization of a project, running a training session and carefully monitoring the activities involved all demand sophisticated professional skills.

Also remember that Cued Spelling can save you time. Close teacher observation during peer tutored CS can prove invaluable for assessment purposes.

Feedback

At the feedback meeting after the six weeks intensive trial period, you will wish to explore the views of pairs on continuing CS. As with PR, if in doubt keep them hungry.

16 Does Cued Spelling Work?

The initial reports on Cued Spelling were descriptive, but nonetheless fascinating. Emerson (1988) reported on a brief project using the technique with four parents who tutored their own children at home. Results at Mastery Review were excellent.

Scoble (1988) reported a detailed case study of an adult literacy student tutored by his wife using the technique. After ten weeks of CS, a Mastery Review of all words covered in the preceding weeks yielded a success rate of 78 per cent.

Subsequently, Scoble (1989) reported on the progress of fourteen similar pairs, most of whom had done Paired Reading together. One student had used the method for over a year and usually achieved Speed Review scores of 100 per cent and Mastery Review scores of 90 per cent. Harrison (1989) reported on a similar project and its extension to peer tutoring between adult literacy students in an evening class.

Peer-tutored Cued Spelling

In the event, however, the most popular application of Cued Spelling proved to be in peer tutoring. Oxley and Topping (1990) reported on a project in which eight seven- and eight-year-old pupils were tutored by eight nine-year-old pupils in the same vertically grouped class in a small rural school.

This cross-age, cross-ability fixed role peer tutoring project was found to yield striking social benefits. The children became more cooperative and self-organizing as a group. Cross-age friendships became much more prevalent. They spontaneously praised each other in many different situations. Without any staff involvement, two tutors initiated a Friendly Patrol in the playground. They awarded stickers for positive social performances, such as being smiley. They also spontaneously generalized peer tutoring to other curriculum areas, such as instrumental music and mathematics, and to other situations, such as with siblings at home.

Subjective feedback from both tutors and tutees was positive. In eight tutorial pairs, all the tutors and six tutees found Cued Spelling easy to learn to do. Two tutees found it hard to think of good words and three found it hard to think of good cues. All eight tutees reported they now felt happier about spelling and now did better at spelling tests. Seven felt they self-corrected more. However, few reported perceiving an improvement in their spelling in the course of free writing. All the tutees said they enjoyed CS but only five of the tutors said this. Five tutees wished to continue with CS but none of the tutors wished to do so.

The self-concept as a speller of both tutees and tutors showed a marked positive shift compared to that of non-participant children, and especially so for the tutees. (This was measured using the Vincent-Claydon Self Concept as a Speller scale.)

After six weeks, a total Mastery Review of all target words yielded average scores of 66 per cent, with great variability between pairs, but a test session of up to 92 items for such young children was considered of doubtful reliability. Also, some of the tutees had frequently chosen words of great difficulty and doubtful utility.

Results on two norm-referenced tests of spelling were equivocal. One test suffered from a ceiling effect with some tutors, and the other from a floor effect with the weakest tutees. Tutees made gains of 2.3 times normal rates, and tutors made gains of 2.8 times normal rates. However, although the scores of both tutees and tutors were strikingly improved at post-test, so were those of non-participant children in the same class.

This may be attributed to format practice effects on the test (parallel forms were used), to the John Henry effect, to contamination between groups, or a combination of factors. This study does demonstrate the importance of having control or comparison groups, however. The correlation between results on the two standardized tests and between those and Mastery Review scores was not high. This perhaps illustrates the desirability of evaluation by 'multiple measures of independent imperfection'.

Peer-tutored Cued Spelling on a larger scale in a class-wide, same-age, same-ability reciprocal tutoring format was reported by Brierley *et al.* (1989). All pupils in three middle school mixed-ability classes (aged 9 to 10) participated. Tutor and tutee roles changed each week. All 75 children were trained in a single group meeting and practiced back in their own classes. This is economical of time but not necessarily recommended.

After six weeks, a total Mastery Review of all words covered yielded average scores of 80 per cent. The highest number of correct spellings at final Mastery Review was 54 and the highest percentage success rate 100 per cent. There are problems in expressing Mastery Review scores in summary form, since neither percentage nor total adequately reflects performance where children are attempting different numbers of target words of varying difficulty. Given this, and other factors, the correlation between Mastery Review scores and norm-referenced test scores may not be high or particularly meaningful. In this study, the correlation was low.

On a norm-referenced spelling test, the average gain for all children was 0.65 years of spelling age during the six-week project, higher than would be expected, despite the ceiling effect artificially depressing the results. The average for one class was 0.47 years gain, for another 0.7. The best individual gain in spelling age was 2.1 years.

Subjective feedback from the children was positive. Ninety per cent felt that Cued Spelling was easy to learn to do. Eighty-four per cent reported feeling happier about spelling in general; 69 per cent said they were better at spelling tests after the project and 65 per cent said their spelling in free writing was better. Eighty-five per cent felt their self-correction had improved. Sixty-six per cent said they liked Cued Spelling. However, only 53 per cent of the children reported finding it easy to think of good cues and only 38 per cent found it easy to think of good target words.

There were striking differences between classes in subjective feedback, including wishes for continuation. In the most enthusiastic class, 39 per cent of the children wished to do Cued Spelling five times a week, another 39 per cent wished to do it twice a week, and 22 per cent wished to carry on with spelling work but in a different way. Across all three classes, however, the average proportion wishing to carry on doing Cued Spelling was 47 per cent. This clearly demonstrates that even with identical initial input, what the coordinating teacher does subsequently in the classroom can make a big difference. However, even the results from the least enthusiastic class were good.

Subsequently, peer-tutored Cued Spelling was initiated by teachers in a number of schools, especially in the reciprocal tutoring format, but few found time to evaluate it.

Parent-tutored Cued Spelling

A study of parent-tutored Cued Spelling with 47 children of eight years of age and of the normal range of spelling ability was undertaken by France *et al.* (1993). This school already had a whole-school spelling policy, all teachers promoted the Look-Cover-Write-Check method and carried out considerable direct teaching on phoneme and morpheme clusters, as well as operating 'sponsored spells' and other related events.

The results indicated that the intervention appeared to be effective in differentially raising the spelling attainments of participants as compared to non-participants who were more able spellers, at least in the short term. A participant sample of 22 children and a non-participant comparison group of ten children in the same class were tested. The Cued Spellers on average gained 0.51 years of spelling age in six weeks while the comparison group gained 0.18 years. (The comparison group tended to be slightly more able spellers at pre-test.) Girls did especially well.

The children felt Cued Spelling was easy to learn to do and that it improved their spelling along a number of dimensions. Sixty-nine per cent reported improved performance on spelling tests and in self-correction, while 74 per cent reported improved spelling in continuous free writing. Eighty-five per cent said they were happier about spelling. Sixty-nine per cent reported it was easy to find cues but 77 per cent found it hard to find good words. However, 62 per cent said they tended to become bored. Nevertheless, 72 per cent said they wanted to go on doing it.

Despite the emphasis on collecting words, parents reported children had not always managed to do this. Other children deliberately chose very hard words and built in failure for themselves, despite being counseled about this. Some children applied phonic cues to words which sounded the same yet had different meanings (homophones), to the discomfiture of the parent tutor. Generally, however, the parents approved of and appreciated the project.

Comparing parent and peer tutoring

It can be argued that any method involving extra time on task at spelling and extra valuable parental attention and approval related to spelling might be likely to yield differential gains. A study by Watt and Topping (1992) compared Cued Spelling with traditional spelling homework (an alternative intervention involving equal tutor attention and equal time on spelling tasks), compared the relative effectiveness of parent- and peer-tutored Cued Spelling, and assessed the generalization of the effect of Cued Spelling into subsequent continuous free writing.

The 23 Cued Spellers gained over two months of spelling age for each calendar month elapsed on one norm-referenced spelling test; a sub-sample showed even larger gains on another test. The traditional spelling homework comparison group of more able spellers gained only half a month of spelling age per calendar month. Parent and peer tutoring seemed equally effective in terms of test gains.

The average score for parent tutored children at final Mastery Review of words used in the program was 93 per cent. The Mastery Reviews were staggered rather than completed at one sitting. Parent and peer tutoring also seemed equally effective in terms of CS words mastered.

Participating children returned questionnaires identical to those used by Oxley and Topping (1990). Of these, 56 per cent found it easy to think up good cues while the rest thought it hard, but 87 per cent now felt happier about spelling in general and that their spelling was better when writing, while 83 per cent felt they now did better at spelling tests. Ninety-one per cent reported a higher rate of self-correction after doing Cued Spelling and the same proportion said they liked doing Cued Spelling, while 87 per cent said they wished to go on doing Cued Spelling.

Parents returned feedback questionnaires and 88 per cent reported a higher rate of self-correction, confirming the feedback from the children, while 58 per cent reported noticing their children spontaneously generalize the use of Cued Spelling techniques to other words. Three of the four teachers involved noted higher rates of self-correction of spelling in class work and a general improvement in free writing.

Pre–post analysis of written work was based on samples of writing from eighteen Cued Spellers and a small number of comparison children. Cued Spellers tended to produce longer pieces of writing after the project compared to before it, and in all but one case the proportional number of misspellings was less, despite evidence of inclusion of more ambitious and exotic vocabulary. The comparison group also tended to produce longer pieces at post-test, but error rate did not show the same decrease. The average number of spelling errors per page reduced from 8.5 to 4.6 for the Cued Spellers and from 3.7 to 2.1 for the comparison children, who clearly had a lower error rate to start with and thus had less room for improvement.

Generally all but one of the participants and all but one of the comparison children were adjudged to have improved in quality of written work (one would of course expect children in school to improve over time). Analysis was based on these categories: detail of language and semantics, vocabulary, structure and planning, spelling, punctuation, repetition and redundancy, complexity of grammar, and accuracy of grammar. However, the CS group recorded an average of 1.7 specific improvements per child while the comparison group averaged 1.2.

This study appears to have shown the superiority of Cued Spelling over traditional spelling homework and weekly spelling tests. Much of the Cued Spelling evaluation literature has been reviewed in Topping (1995d).

Summary

The research on Cued Spelling is much less voluminous than that on Paired Reading. Although the Cued Spelling research has included control or comparison groups and has checked generalization of gains into other contexts, there is as yet little longer-term follow-up evidence. Studies of this kind are needed.

Nevertheless, the picture to date is very positive. Cued Spelling seems to improve self-esteem. Both parent- and peer-tutored Cued Spelling has led to average gains on standardized spelling tests of 4.1 times normal expectations (range 2.2 to 5.0). Mastery Review at project end shows average retention of 82 per cent of target words (range 66 per cent to 93 per cent).

The majority of children find Cued Spelling easy to learn to do. After Cued Spelling, a majority report that they feel happier about spelling (84 per cent to 100 per cent) and are better at self-correcting (69 per cent to 91 per cent) and spelling tests (69 per cent to 100 per cent). A smaller majority report perceiving generalized improvement in spelling in free writing (average 68 per cent, range 24 per cent to 87 per cent). Most children say they wish to carry on doing Cued Spelling (47 per cent to 87 per cent).

Difficulties encountered by some children are finding good target words (range 25 per cent to 77 per cent) and thinking up good cues (range 31 per cent to 47 per cent). This clearly highlights the need for Cued Spelling projects to give special emphasis to these organizational aspects.

A summary of the CS research will be found on overhead masters on the TRW website.

17 How To Evaluate Cued Spelling

As with all evaluation, this should be conducted with reference to the objectives set for the project, which may be academic, affective, social, or a combination of these. The discussion of research designs for Paired Reading applies here also (reading Chapter 5 before this chapter will be very helpful). Measures will of course be different.

Criterion-referenced assessment

Cued Spelling does of course have its own evaluation system inbuilt in the form of Mastery Reviews. This is a form of curriculum-based or criterion-referenced test that is individualized to each child. You should aggregate the scores from weekly Mastery Reviews. These are readily obtainable from the CS Diaries.

Many project coordinators also conduct total Mastery Reviews at the end of the intensive period on all of the CS words worked with over this period, as a check on longer-term retention. Some children will have worked on a very large number of words and you may need to stagger these total Mastery Reviews in sections, otherwise the children will be overwhelmed. You should anticipate an average score of 80 per cent correct on this total Mastery Review if the project has worked satisfactorily. A further longer-term follow-up some weeks after the intensive period would be a valuable check on even longer retention.

Cued Spelling does of course seek to do more than help children remember a number of difficult words. It also aims to improve general spelling skills. Therefore, evaluation efforts should examine the generalization of improved spelling skills to new words never the subject of Cued Spelling activity, and to new contexts outside the framework of CS, e.g. continuous free writing.

Criterion-referenced spelling tests intended to check generalization of improved spelling skills can be constructed of words considered developmentally appropriate, words of high frequency of use, words commonly spelled wrongly, words drawn from or exemplifying other direct teaching of spelling, or essential vocabulary in other curriculum areas. Many traditional weekly spelling tests given to the whole class were informally constructed in this way.

However, if such a measure is to be applied on a pre–post basis, keeping the content identical on both occasions is likely to result in content practice effects (so a control group would be highly desirable). Changing the content would raise grave doubts about the comparability of the two forms (so a control group would be highly desirable).

Norm-referenced tests

A number of standardized (norm-referenced) spelling tests have been used to evaluate the generalization of Cued Spelling gains to completely new words. This can be related to normal expectations and/or (preferably) to the performance of an equivalent control or comparison group.

In fixed role tutoring, the gains of the tutors as well as those of the tutees can be assessed and compared. In reciprocal role tutoring, everyone will have been both tutor and tutee, so this comparison will not be possible.

There are many fewer standardized tests of spelling than of reading, and in many countries there are no standardized tests available in the first language of the country. Where standardized tests are available, they vary greatly from country to country and such tests can go out of date quite quickly. Consequently, those wishing to use such tests would do better to scrutinize the catalogs of the major educational test suppliers in their country (most of which are now available on-line) or access more general compendiums of tests, such as the Buros database of mental measurements (also now available on-line). The latter reports on freely available public domain tests as well as commercially available tests.

Some spelling tests (e.g. the Vincent and Claydon) include measures of self-esteem as a speller and these enable the comparison of before and after project scores and contrast with a non-participant group if possible.

Attitudinal gains may also be found with respect to liking spelling itself, liking other related curricular areas, liking peer tutoring per se irrespective of content, and so on. Social gains may be explored via questionnaire, sociometry or observation. You may wish to see whether the project has resulted in greater social interaction outside and beyond tutoring sessions across genders, social class, ethnic grouping, age group, ability group, and so on.

Subjective feedback

Reproducible specimen Evaluation Questionnaires for subjective feedback from peer or parent tutors and from tutees will be found on the TRW website. These offer a quick and easy way of obtaining consumer feedback which is readily summarized.

Generalization to writing

Attempts to analyse free writing for better spelling are problematic. As the Watt and Topping (1993) study showed, assessing the application of CS to continuous free writing outside the CS framework is complex and time-consuming. However, it is fascinating if you can spare the time.

Just as with Paired Reading, if a simple error count is used on a before and after basis, this takes no account of tutees becoming more ambitious. If post-project they are trying to spell harder words, they may make as many errors as before but at a higher level.

Some sort of allowance for difficulty might be considered, perhaps involving before and after comparison of error rate in bands of two-syllable words, three-syllable words, four-syllable words, and so on. This would offer only the crudest of indices, however.

Other assessments of the general quality of free writing are discussed in Part Three. There is certainly scope for creative invention in the evaluation of the impact of Cued Spelling, or indeed any other spelling intervention.

Part Five
Development and Resources

18 Sustained Gains: Embedding Paired Learning

Education suffers from short-lived initiatives that enjoy a brief period of being fashionable, then fall out of favor and disappear without trace. It is worrying that some of these initiatives seem to become fashionable even though there is no evidence for their effectiveness. It is even more worrying that some seem to go out of fashion even when there is good evidence that they are effective.

So, you have successfully completed a first Paired Reading, Paired Thinking, Paired Writing or Cued Spelling project. You have seen worthwhile improvement in a majority of your students and are feeling pleased with yourself. Great! Now it is time to think about consolidation – embedding Paired Learning within the school organization so that it continues to maximize student potential, enduring through whatever political, financial, sociological or other tides that might flow your way – and preferably making it so widespread, durable and embedded in the system that it will endure long after you have left the school.

In addition to embedding Paired Learning as part of continuing mainstream practice, you will wish to consider extending it to:

- more helpers and helped
- helpers and helped with greater difficulties
- other subject areas
- other classes and colleagues
- other PL methods.

The potential is enormous. But as ever, remember that a modest development done well is better than a large development done badly.

Reaching the hard-to-reach

In peer tutoring programs, the raw material is always to hand (except for children who truant, but even they often turn up for their peer tutoring session). Parent tutoring or family literacy programs can have much larger recruitment problems, especially in disadvantaged areas.

Of course, some of those in need will remain unreachable, at least for now. Families who have not enjoyed a good relationship with school in the past will naturally be suspicious.

However, schools that can offer a more or less failure-free method of known cost-effectiveness have inherent marketing advantages. They can say things such as 'Come to school for a one hour meeting and we will show you how at home in just five minutes a day for five days a week you can almost certainly make your child a much better reader'.

Furthermore, they can say this confident that experience and research back them up, confident that the first graduates of the program will spread the good news around the neighborhood, confident that once some momentum builds the problem may be meeting all the demand.

They can also say this knowing that while the major marketing thrust may be in terms of parents helping children, which is highly socially acceptable, once a family has been empowered all kinds of other tutoring arrangements will spring up, truly embodying the full concept of paired learning.

In many cases the school will never know about these. They will involve that vast majority of low literacy adults who hide their problem away and will never come to a regular adult class. Paired learning activities are a highly potent means of involving disaffected low literacy adults. For many, reading with their child is the only way of socially legitimizing reading books of low readability and child-like content. For many, 'helping' their child is their only motivation to read.

However, we will never reach all the families we would wish. Paradoxically, a school operating a successful parent-tutored Paired Learning program can place the disadvantaged children who are left out in a still worse position relative to those who are participating in the program. This is of course where peer tutoring in school comes to the rescue.

Many teachers feel compelled to arrange alternative extra support for the most needy non-participant children, perhaps via volunteer adults coming into school or by giving up their own break time to act as surrogate parents. However, the organizational complexity of maintaining a reliable rota of volunteer adults who are available often enough to actually make a difference to the child's attainment should not be underestimated. The teacher's own time is much too valuable to be used in this way.

Peer tutoring is the obvious answer. If appropriate methods are deployed, both tutees and tutors gain in attainment, the tutors 'learning by teaching'.

Developing a whole school approach

There is no better apprenticeship for being a helper than being helped. Many schools with cross-year class-wide peer tutor programs actively promote the equal opportunity and apprenticeship advantages of this model. Every student who is helped in a lower grade fully expects from the outset to become a tutor when in a higher grade. As students are helped in preparation for becoming helpers, any ambivalence about receiving help decreases and motivation to learn often increases. The asymmetry between helper and helped is reduced, and the stigma often otherwise associated with receiving help disappears. All the students have the chance to participate and the opportunity to help, which makes them all feel equally valuable and worthwhile.

Sometimes students who are helped in one subject are simultaneously helpers to students in a lower grade in the same subject. Those who are helped in one subject may be helpers to their own age peers in another subject. Even the most able student in any grade can be presented with problems that require the help of an even more capable student from a higher grade, and thereby learn that no one is as smart as all of us. The symbiosis of the helper and helped roles is something upon which to consciously capitalize.

Over time a critical mass of teachers who support Paired Learning can develop in the school, although a few colleagues may always have difficulty adapting to the role of manager of flexible and effective learning rather than that of direct transmitter of traditional wisdom.

PL builds on students' strengths and mobilizes them as active participants in the learning process. Not only do helpers learn the subject better and more deeply, but they also learn transferable skills in helping and cooperation, listening and communication. All of this influences the school ethos, developing a cultural norm of helping and caring. PL contributes to a sense of cohesive community and encourages personal and social development. Eventually, Paired Learning can permeate the whole ethos of a school and be deployed spontaneously in many areas of the curriculum.

Although every working day they are part of a very busy community, teachers all too often feel strangely isolated. Finding time together to have a discussion is difficult enough, and at the end of the school day energies are at a low ebb. Ideally, time should be scheduled to bring teachers together regularly in mutual support and problem-solving gatherings where they can share their ideas, materials and methods, and build each other's confidence and self-esteem. Paired Learning works very well with teachers, too.

Another problem arises from changes of professional personnel. Frequently the teacher who is first to innovate within a school is also the teacher who is offered promotion soonest, which may take them to another district or school, a gain for the receiving school, but a serious loss for the previous school. Arranging for skills to be passed on before innovators depart is essential to manage human resources effectively.

These difficulties hinder attempts to develop all coordinated whole school developments, of course, not only Paired Learning. While forward planning and energy are needed to overcome them, the rewards are great.

Ensuring sustained success

How are we to ensure the longer term success of PL strategies? Embedding PL within an organization or larger community requires careful attention to the needs of the learners, the professional educators, and the wider system. In order for a PL initiative to survive and grow, there are some considerations that should be met. If you want your Paired Learning initiative to last and/or spread, consider the following:

Cost-benefit balance for all

The benefits must outweigh the costs for all concerned if the initiative is to endure. For the initiating teacher, costs will be in terms of time, materials and other resources, and the general harassment and stress involved in doing anything new. On the benefit side, the teacher will need both subjective and objective evidence of impact in relation to the objectives set.

More than that, the initiative also has to feel good – have a warm and satisfying social and emotional tone. This requires deliberate cultivation. However, no teacher is an island, and the initiative also needs to be compatible with the current local philosophy, political correctness and mood of the professional peer group and senior policy dictators. Fortunately, Paired Learning has largely escaped adverse politicization – it is right up there with motherhood and apple pie in terms of acceptability.

A similar analysis can be applied to the other participants – the helpers, the helped students, and the school principal. All need minimization of time wastage and harassment, need to feel good about the project, need to be clear what they are getting out of it and what the other participants are getting out of it, and need to be able to confidently assert their support for it in the face of possible disbelief from their peer group.

Objectives and applications

Be clear about the different objectives for different types of Paired Learning. Your objectives for a specific project may be in the cognitive, affective or social domain, or some combination. Don't let someone else evaluate your project against a different set of objectives!

Choose your format to suit your context, objectives and possibilities. Consider which formats will suit which subjects, topics, activities, classes, and so on. Use a mixture of cross-age and same-age, cross-ability and same-ability, fixed role and reciprocal role methods as necessary and optimal.

Plan for flexibility. If you work at it you can figure out a format or method that will fit into almost any local exigency: complex organizations, highly structured schedules, lack of physical space, lack of appropriate furniture, poor acoustics, rigid attitudes in adults in positions of power, rigid attitudes in children who have learned to prefer inertia, and so on. But don't be too ambitious to start with. Many small steps get you there quickest in the end.

Materials, methods and monitoring

Materials should preferably be low cost, already to hand, differentiated for different needs, attractive and durable. A simple system for access to and exchange of the necessary materials is needed. Tracking current possession of items may be necessary, but don't get hung up with bureaucracy that makes work.

Prescribe a clear and simple method for interaction to start with. Ensure the participants always receive good quality training. Remember methods need to be truly and consistently interactive, or one partner will go to sleep. Ensure the method involves modeling as well as discussion, questioning and explaining. Ensure there are clear procedures for the identification, diagnosis and correction of errors.

Ensure the method builds in and capitalizes on intrinsic satisfaction for all participants. Once the participants are experiencing success, ensure they do not become dependent on a routine method. Make clear the times and opportunities within which they are encouraged and even required to be creative and to take the initiative.

Close monitoring of participant behavior is especially necessary at the beginning, where student deviation can lead to failure which will be attributed to you. After an initial period of 'getting it right', creative and reflective deviance in students may be encouraged, but will need close monitoring. In the longer run, some 'drift' is almost inevitable. Keep checking to see that it is productive.

Rejuvenation, evaluation and iteration

Initiating a project (especially in an inert environment) is very demanding in terms of time and energy, although that capital investment is almost always considered worthwhile later. Once things are up and running smoothly, it is tempting to either relax, or rush on and start another project with a different group. The latter is more dangerous than the former. Don't spread yourself too thinly. After a few weeks or months most initiatives need some rejuvenation, not necessarily an organizational improvement, just a change to inject some novelty.

Fortunately, Paired Learning is very flexible and offers many ways for injecting variety and novelty – change of partners, subject topics or activities, format of operation, and so on. However, please do not try to use it for everything or you will overwhelm the learners. It can enhance productivity to give them a rest and then return to a modified format not too long afterwards. In any event, close consultation with the students always adds extra momentum to their motivation. Even if their suggestions are contradictory and cannot all be implemented, the feeling that their views are valued increases commitment to the onward process.

Projects must target gains for all participants (particularly the helpers). Evaluation should also seek to check whether there are longer-term as well as short-term gains, and whether helping generalizes outside the specifically nominated PL sessions.

You may wish to consider to what extent you can give away some of the organization and management to the participants themselves. Obviously you need to check on this from time to time, especially with younger children. Of course, you wish positives to be accentuated and negatives to be eliminated. Keeping the feel good factor going is important. However, a degree of self-management (which can include self-monitoring) can heighten self-esteem and responsibility and help to make initiatives self-sustaining.

Once Paired Learning is accepted and deployed by more staff, some coordination will be necessary. Working together, you can build iterative cycles of involvement in different kinds of Paired Learning in different formats with all children in role as helpers and as helped at different times, in a developmental progressive sequence.

Beyond this, however, are the systemic implications of frequent, various and equal opportunities for all to be both helper and helped. These lead to a positive ethos in which Paired Learning is accepted as something normal permeating everyday life, a learning tool as natural as opening a book or turning on a computer. When you see your students explaining to a newcomer from another district what Paired Learning is all about, and showing amazement on discovering that everybody doesn't do it everywhere, you will know you have got it embedded.

A warning about customization

Enthusiastic teachers often want to customize or adapt methods, to suit their own classroom or children. The materials on the TRW website are deliberately made available electronically so that they can be customized to local needs. However, a word of warning is needed. It is only the structured methods described here that have been evaluated. If you customize so enthusiastically that your method no longer bears much relationship to the original, you cannot expect automatic transfer of effectiveness.

Sometimes these adaptations can be extremely successful, sometimes not. Either way, they can make extra work for busy teachers. Also, by the time the adapted method has been passed on repeatedly by word of mouth, the multiple changes eventually result in something totally unlike the original method. But if the highly diluted adaptation is found to be ineffective, the original method still tends to be blamed. For all of these reasons, we suggest that – at least for your first venture into this field – you keep to the guidelines outlined in this book. You still need to make many professional decisions about what is best for your own class and your own children.

As and when you do customize, you will need to put extra effort into the evaluation of your new method.

The value of evaluation

What are you going to do with your evaluation results? Feeding general data on their success back to the participants may well increase their longer-term motivation. Publicizing the data may expand subsequent recruitment or attract additional funding. But how will you review to what extent the curriculum content of the activity has actually been mastered and retained in the longer term?

Follow-up evaluation to assess the maintenance of short-term gains is important. You will need to build in some means for continuing review, feedback and injection of further novelty and enthusiasm. Otherwise all pairs will not automatically keep going and maintain the use of their skills. Again, the social dynamic of the group is important. You need to use this positively. Evidence on the generalization of gains to other contexts and other curriculum areas is also important. You are likely also to need to consciously foster participants' broadening the use of their new skills to different materials and contexts for new purposes. All of this will consolidate the progress made, build confidence and empower the pair still further.

When pairs have developed sufficient awareness of effective tutoring to begin to design their own systems, you know you have done a good job. As tutees themselves recruit a wider range of tutors, the tutee becomes even more central as quality controller of the tutoring process.

New applications: the example of Paired Reading

Paired Reading started life as a method designed for weaker readers, then quickly became a method offered on an equal opportunity basis to readers of all abilities, including adults. It started in the UK, but has spread to many parts of the world and is now widely used in developed countries (e.g. within the US in volunteer tutoring schemes) and also in countries with development needs (e.g. within family literacy programs in the townships of South Africa and in provincial parts of Brazil).

In more advantaged countries, PR is connecting with the development of electronic literacy. It can be used with material on the World Wide Web, or with a shared story loaded into an Ebook. Stemming from its reincarnation as Duolog Reading in the US, PR is also linking to software for computerized self-assessment of reading comprehension of real books by children – an excellent additional form of motivation, monitoring and accountability for both members of a peer tutoring pair.

As we have seen, PR can be deployed to help address concerns about the under-achievement of boys in reading. It can also be deployed to support the transition from primary school to high school both socially and academically, and has featured in many literacy summer schools. It can also be deployed to address issues of equal opportunities and social inclusion, social competence and school ethos, especially in schools where different year groups, classes or other groups do not customarily relate well.

Over the years it has proved to be an extraordinarily flexible method. In the UK, it fits into the current National Literacy Strat-

egy. Indeed, it fits into most strategies, and has proven to be philo-
sophically and ethically acceptable by very diverse teachers who may
not agree on anything else. There are undoubtedly many new applications still waiting to be found.

With a thorough understanding of the basic principles of engi-
neering for Paired Learning, you can begin to design projects and
programs specifically tailored to your own neighborhood and classroom. Further discussion of the principles involved in Designing
New Paired Methods will be found on the TRW website (General
section). Good luck with your efforts.

Resources: TRW website

The reproducible resources which accompany this book are made available electronically via the World Wide Web. This enables the provision of a much larger number of resources (over 60), and reduces the cost of the book. It also enables users to customize resources to their own requirements, and the easy addition of new resources as they are developed.

If you do not have ready access to the World Wide Web, visit your local public library, where they will assist you.

The resources will be found on the TRW website at the author's university (www.dundee.ac.uk/psychology/TRW).

The resources are available to read immediately online in your web browser. These html files can also be saved to your own hard disc, floppy or other portable disc, or to a network file space (using the File menu, Save As command), and opened and read later in your browser. If you try to open the html file in your word processor, you may be offered a conversion of the file to the format of your word processor. You can also select the text you require on the browser screen and copy and paste it into your preferred word processor. Remember, you might have to adjust the page size and set-up.

However, the latter two operations are not always successful in files that are in table form or have other complex layouts. You may find that the formatting and layout have been disrupted by the transfer. Therefore, for browser files that are likely to be disrupted in this way, you will find a link to download the file in other formats.

The Resources are organized in sections parallel to the parts of the TRW book to which they relate (see below). They are prefaced by a section on more general resources to do with peer, parent and volunteer tutoring.

Within each section, the resources available from the TRW website are followed by other relevant resources from elsewhere. The resources from elsewhere include video and other multimedia content as well as web-based resources. Some are free, some are not.

Resource Menu

Choose from:

- General
- Paired Reading Resources
- Paired Thinking Resources
- Paired Writing Resources
- Cued Spelling Resources.

List of Resources on TRW Website

General
Peer Assisted Learning: Information for Parents
Dictionary of Praise (cross-reference to)
Planning Proformas (cross-reference to)
Designing New Paired Methods

Paired Reading
PR How To Do It (for Parent Tutors)
PR How To Do It (for Peer Tutors)
PR Method Overhead Masters (for Parents)
PR Flowchart
PR Advantages
PR Planning Proforma – Peer Tutoring
PR Planning Proforma – Parent Tutoring
PR Technique Checklist
PR Diary
PR Dictionary of Praise
PR Certificate of Merit
PR Beyond Paired Reading Handout
PR Literature Review to 1995
PR Research Overhead Masters
PR Evaluation Questionnaire (for Tutees)
PR Evaluation Questionnaire (for Parent Tutors)

PR Evaluation Questionnaire (for Peer Tutors)
PR Evaluation Questionnaire (for Teachers, re individual child)
PR Evaluation Questionnaire (for Teachers, re whole class)

Paired Thinking

PT Structure: Summary
PT Tips for Peer or Parent Tutors (in full)
PT Tips for Peer or Parent Tutors (reminders)
PT Level 1 Prompt Sheet
PT Level 2 Prompt Sheet
PT Level 3 Prompt Sheet
PT Level 4 Prompt Sheet
PT Technique Checklist
PT Evaluation Questionnaire (for Tutees)
PT Evaluation Questionnaire (for Tutors)
PT Evaluation Questionnaire (for Teachers)

Paired Writing

PW Flowchart
PW Method Overhead Masters
PW Drafting Support Stages
PW Editing and Evaluation Reminder Sheet
PW Self and Peer Evaluation Forms
PW Technique Checklist
PW Teacher Peer Tutoring Role Reminder Sheet
PW Emergent Writing Evaluation Questionnaire (for Teachers)
PW Evaluation Questionnaire (for Tutees and Peer or Parent Tutors)
PW Evaluation Interview Schedule (for Peer Tutors)
PW Evaluation Interview Schedule (for Peer Tutees)
PW Evaluation Interview Schedule (for Teachers)

Cued Spelling

CS Flowchart
CS Diary Sheet
CS Mnemonic Strategies Handout
CS Mnemonic Ideas Handout
CS How To Do It
CS Abbreviated Procedure

CS Research Overhead Masters
CS Evaluation Questionnaire (for Peer or Parent Tutors)
CS Evaluation Questionnaire (for Tutees)

References

Many other references about Paired Reading up to 1995 can be found on the 'PR Literature Review To 1995' resource on the TRW website.

The Paired Reading Bulletins and Paired Learning are available internationally from the Educational Resources Information Center (ERIC) through any library (microfiche reference numbers: 1985 – ED 2285124; 1986 – ED 285125; 1987 – ED 285126; 1988 – ED 298429; 1989 – ED 313656).

Adey, P. and Shayer, M. (1994) *Really Raising Standards: Cognitive Intervention and Academic Achievement*. London: Routledge.

Bangert-Drowns, R. L. and Bankert, E. (1990) *Meta-analysis of Effects of Explicit Instruction for Critical Thinking*. (ERIC Document Reproduction Service No. ED 328 614).

Barrett, W. L. (1999) *Qualitative Evaluation of Paired Thinking through Circle Time at Langlees Primary School*. Dundee: Centre for Paired Learning, University of Dundee.

Baumann, J. F., Seifert-Kessell, N. and Jones, L. A. (1992) Effect of think-aloud instruction on elementary students' comprehension monitoring abilities. *Journal of Reading Behavior*, 24, 143–72.

Beck, I. L., McKeown, M. G., Hamilton, R. L. and Kucan, L. (1997) *Questioning the Author: Student Engagement with Text*. Newark, DE: International Reading Association.

Blagg, N. (1991) *Can We Teach Intelligence?: A Comprehensive Evaluation of Feuerstein's Instrumental Enrichment Programme*. London: Erlbaum.

Block, C. C. (1993) Strategy instruction in a literature-based reading program. *Elementary School Journal*, 94 (2), 139–51.

Bottomley, D., Henk, W. A. and Melnick, S. A. (1997) Assessing children's views about themselves as writers using the Writer Self-Perception Scale. *Reading Teacher*, 51 (4), 286–94.

Bowers, D. (1991) Using peer tutoring as a form of individualized instruction for the at-risk students in a regular classroom. Fort Lauderdale, FL: Nova University. (ERIC Document Reproduction Service No. ED 331 631).

Bratcher, S. (1994) *Evaluating Children's Writing: A Handbook of Communication Choices for Classroom Teachers*. Hillsdale, NJ: Erlbaum.

Brierley, M., Hutchinson, P., Topping, K. and Walker, C. (1989) Reciprocal peer tutored Cued Spelling with ten year olds. *Paired Learning*, 5, 136–40.

Brimer, A. (1969) *Bristol Achievement Tests*. Windsor: NFER-Nelson.

Brooks, G., Flanagan, N., Henkhuzens, Z. and Hutchison, D. (1998) *What Works for Slow Readers? The Effectiveness of Early Intervention Schemes*. Slough: National Foundation for Educational Research.

Brown, R., Pressley, M., Van Meter, P. and Schuder, T. (1996) A quasi-experimental validation of Transactional Strategies Instruction with low-achieving second-grade readers. *Journal of Educational Psychology*, 88, 18–37.

Carlson, D. M. and Roellich, C. (1983) Teaching writing easily and effectively to get results. Part 2: The evaluation process. Paper presented at annual meeting of the National Council of Teachers of English, Seattle, WA, April 14–16. (ERIC Document Reproduction Service No. ED 233 372).

Carr, E. and Allen, J. (1987) Peer teaching and learning during writing time in kindergarten. Paper presented at the National Reading Conference, St. Petersburg FL, December.

Coles, M. J. and Robinson, W. D. (eds.) (1991) *Teaching Thinking: A Survey of Programmes in Education*. London: Bristol Classical Press.

Cooper, C. R. (1977) Holistic evaluation of writing. In C. R. Cooper and L. Odell (eds.), *Evaluating Writing: Describing, Measuring, Judging*. Buffalo, NY: SUNY Press and National Council of Teachers of English.

Cupolillo, M., Silva, R. S., Socorro, S. and Topping, K. J. (1997) Paired reading with Brazilian first-year school failures. *Educational Psychology in Practice*, 13 (2), 96–100.

Daiute, C. (1989) Play as thought: thinking strategies of young writers. *Harvard Educational Review*, 59 (1), 1–23.

Daiute, C. (1990) The role of play in writing development. *Research in the Teaching of English*, 24 (1), 4–47.

Daiute, C. and Dalton, B. (1993) Collaboration between children learning to write: can novices be masters? *Cognition and Instruction*, 10 (4), 281–333.

Davies, F. and Greene, T. (1981) Directed activities related to text: Text analysis and text reconstruction. Paper presented at the annual meeting of the International Reading Association, New Orleans, April 27–May 1. (ERIC Document Reproduction Service No. ED 208 386).

DeAngelo, N. (1997) *Improving Reading Achievement Through the Use of Parental Involvement and Paired Reading.* Chicago: Saint Xavier University. (ERIC Document Reproduction Service No. ED 409 536).

DeBono, E. (1990) *Lateral Thinking: Creativity Step-by-Step.* London: HarperCollins.

DeGroff, L. (1992) Process-writing: teachers' responses to fourth-grade writers' first drafts. *Primary School Journal*, 93 (2), 131–44.

Diederich, P. (1974) *Measuring Growth in English.* Urbana IL: National Council of Teachers of English.

Dyson, A. H. (1993) *Social Worlds of Children Learning to Write in an Urban Primary School.* New York: Teachers College Press.

Dyson, A. H. (1995) Writing children: reinventing the development of childhood literacy. *Written Communication*, 12, 4–46.

Elliott, J. A. and Hewison, J. (1994) Comprehension and interest in home reading. *British Journal of Educational Psychology*, 64, 203–20.

Elliott, J., Arthurs, J. and Williams, R. (2000) Volunteer support in the classroom: the long-term impact of one initiative upon children's reading performance. *British Educational Research Journal*, 26 (2), 227–44.

Emerson, P. (1988) Parent tutored Cued Spelling in a primary school. *Paired Reading Bulletin*, 4, 91–2.

Englert, C. S. and Raphael, T. E. (1988). Constructing well-formed prose: process, structure and metacognitive knowledge. *Exceptional Children*, 54 (6), 513–20.

Fine, E. S. (1989) Collaborative writing: key to unlocking the silences of children. *Language Arts*, 66 (5), 501–8.

Fisher, R. (1990) *Teaching Children to Think.* Oxford: Blackwell.

Fisher, R. (1996) *Stories for Thinking.* Oxford: Nash Pollock.

France, L., Topping, K. and Revell, K. (1993) Parent tutored Cued Spelling. *Support for Learning*, 8 (1), 11–15.

Fuchs, L. S., Fuchs, D., Kazdan, S. and Allen, S. (1999) Effects of peer-assisted learning strategies in reading with and without training in elaborated help giving. *Elementary School Journal*, 99, 201–20.

Fukkink, R., Van der Linden, S., Vosse, A. and Vaessen, K. (1997) *Handleiding Stap Door*. Utrecht: Sardes.

Gambrell, L. B. and Alamasi, J. F. (1996) *Lively Discussions! Fostering Engaged Reading*. Newark, DE: International Reading Association.

Gambrell, L. B., Palmer, B. M., Codling, R. M. and Mazzoni, S. A. (1996) Assessing motivation to read. *Reading Teacher*, 49 (7), 518–33.

Garcia-Moriyon, F., Colom, R., Lora, S., Rivas, M. and Traver, V. (2000) Evaluation of Philosophy for Children: a program of learning thinking skills. *Psicothema*, 12, 567–71.

Glover, J. and Gary, A. L. (1976) Procedures to increase some aspects of creativity. *Journal of Applied Behavior Analysis*, 9, 79–84.

Goodman, L., Casciato, D. and Price, M. (1987) LD students' writing: analyzing errors. *Academic Therapy*, 22 (5), 453–61.

Gorman, T. and Brooks, G. (1996) *Assessing Young Children's Writing*. London: Basic Skills Agency.

Graham, S. and Harris, K. R. (1989) Improving learning disabled students' skills at composing essays: self-instructional strategy training. *Exceptional Children*, 56 (3), 201–14.

Gustafson, D. J. and Pederson, J. E. (1985) SQ3R: Surveying and questioning the relevant, recent (and not so recent) research. Paper presented at the annual meeting of the Great Lakes Regional Conference of the International Reading Association, Milwaukee, October 17–19. (ERIC Document Reproduction Service No. ED 269 736).

Haggard, M. R. (1988) Developing critical thinking with the directed reading-thinking activity. *Reading Teacher*, 41, 526–33.

Halpern, D. (1998) Teaching critical thinking for transfer across domains: dispositions, skills, structure training and metacognitive monitoring. *American Psychologist*, 53 (4), 449–55.

Hammill, D. and Larsen, D. (1983) *Test of Written Language*. Austin TX: Pro-Ed.

Hannon, P. (1987) A study of the effects of parental involvement in the teaching of reading on children's reading test performance. *British Journal of Educational Psychology*, 57 (1), 56–72.

Harrison, R. (1989) Cued Spelling in adult literacy in Kirklees. *Paired Learning*, 5, 141.

Harrop, A. and McCann, C. (1984) Modifying creative writing in the classroom. *British Journal of Educational Psychology*, 54, 62–72.

Henk, W. A. and Melnick, S. A. (1995) The Reader Self-Perception Scale (RSPS): a new tool for measuring how children feel about themselves as readers. *Reading Teacher*, 48 (6), 470–82.

Hewison, J. (1988) The long term effectiveness of parental involvement in reading: a follow-up to the Haringey Reading Project. *British Journal of Educational Psychology*, 58, 184–90.

Hewison, J. and Tizard, J. (1980) Parental involvement and reading attainment. *British Journal of Educational Psychology*, 50, 209–15.

Hopman, M. and Glynn, T. (1988) Behavioural approaches to improving written expression. *Educational Psychology*, 8 (1/2), 81–100.

Hopman, M. and Glynn, T. (1989) The effect of correspondence training on the rate and quality of written expression of four low achieving boys. *Educational Psychology*, 9 (3), 197–213.

Isaacson, S. (1988) Assessing the writing product: qualitative and quantitative measures. *Exceptional Children*, 54 (6), 528–34.

Jacobs, S. S. (1999) The equivalence of forms A and B of the California Critical Thinking Skills Test. *Measurement and Evaluation in Counseling and Development*, 31 (4), 211–22.

Karegianes, M. L., Pascarella, E. T. and Pflaum, S. W. (1980) The effects of peer editing on the writing proficiency of low-achieving tenth grade students. *Journal of Educational Research*, 73 (4), 203–7.

King, A. (1997) ASK your partner to think – TEL WHY: a model of transactive peer tutoring for scaffolding higher-level complex learning. *Educational Psychologist*, 32, 221–35.

King, A. (1999) Discourse patterns for mediating peer learning. In A. M. O'Donnell and A. King (eds.), *Cognitive Perspectives on Peer Learning*. Mahwah, NJ: Erlbaum.

King, A., Staffieri, A. and Adelgais, A. (1998) Effects of structuring tutorial interaction to scaffold peer learning. *Journal of Educational Psychology*, 90 (1), 134–52.

Klingner, J. K. and Vaughn, S. (1999) Promoting reading comprehension, content learning, and English acquisition through Collaborative Strategic Reading (CSR). *Reading Teacher*, 52 (7), 738–47.

Kopfstein, R. W. (1982) SQ3R doesn't work, or does it? Paper presented at the Annual Meeting of the Western College Reading

Association, San Diego, CA, April 1–4. (ERIC Document Reproduction Service No. ED 216 327).

Kuykendall, C. (1975) Grammar and composition: myths and realities. *English Journal*, 64, 6–7.

Lagana, J. R. (1972) The development, implementation and evaluation of a model for teaching composition which utilizes individualized learning and peer grouping. Unpublished Ph.D. Thesis, University of Pittsburgh.

Law, M. and Kratochwill, T. R. (1993) Paired Reading: an evaluation of a parent tutorial program. *School Psychology International*, 14, 119–47.

Leach, C. (1993) The effect of a Paired Reading program on reading achievement and attitude in a third grade classroom. Wayne, NJ: William Paterson College. (ERIC Document Reproduction Service No. ED 358 424).

Lim, T. K. (1995) An approach to the evaluation of the Philosophy for Children program. *Journal of Cognitive Education*, 4 (2), 89–101.

Lipman, M. (1984) The cultivation of reasoning through philosophy. *Educational Leadership*, 42 (2), 51–6.

MacArthur, C. A. (1999) Overcoming barriers to writing: computer support for basic writing skills. *Reading and Writing Quarterly*, 15 (2), 169–92.

MacArthur, C. and Graham, S. (1987) Learning disabled students' composing under three methods of text production: handwriting, word processing and dictation. *Journal of Special Education*, 21, 22–42.

McGuinness, C. (1999) From thinking skills to thinking classrooms: a review and evaluation of approaches for developing pupils' thinking. Research Report No. 115. London: Stationery Office (for the Department for Education and Employment).

McKenna, M. C. and Kear, D. J. (1990) Measuring attitude toward reading: the Elementary Reading Attitude Survey. *Reading Teacher*, 43 (8), 636–9.

McKenna, M. C. and Kear, D. J. (1995) Garfield revisited: Continued permission to use the ERAS. *Reading Teacher*, 49 (4), 332.

McKinstery, J. and Topping, K. J. Cross-age peer tutoring of thinking skills in the high school. Paper submitted for publication.

Mastropieri, M. A. and Scruggs, T. (2000) Can middle school students with serious reading difficulties help each other and learn anything? Qualitative and quantitative outcomes of a peer tutoring investigation. Paper presented at the annual meeting of the American Educational Research Association, New Orleans, LA, 24–28 April.

Mayfield, M. (1987) *Thinking for Yourself: Developing Critical Thinking Skills Through Writing.* Belmont CA: Wadsworth.

Miller, B. V. and Kratochwill, T. R. (1996) An evaluation of the Paired Reading program using competency-based training. *School Psychology International*, 17, 269–91.

Murad, C. R. and Topping, K. J. (2000) Parents as reading tutors for first graders in Brazil. *School Psychology International*, 21 (2), 152–71.

Nelson, C. (1994) Critical thinking and collaborative learning. In K. Bosworth and S. J. Hamilton (eds.), *Collaborative Learning: Underlying Processes and Effective Techniques.* San Francisco: Jossey-Bass.

Nickerson, R. S. (1988) On improving thinking through instruction. *Review of Research in Education*, 15, 3–57.

Niklasson, J., Ohlsson, R. and Ringborg, M. (1996) Evaluating Philosophy for Children. *Thinking: The Journal of Philosophy for Children*, 12 (4), 17–23.

Nisbet, J. and Davies, P. (1990) The curriculum redefined: learning to think, thinking to learn. *Research Papers in Education*, 5, 49–72.

Nixon, J. and Topping, K. J. (2000) Emergent writing: the impact of structured peer interaction. *Educational Psychology*, 21 (1), 41–58.

Norris, S. P. and Ennis, R. H. (1989) *Evaluating Critical Thinking.* Pacific Grove, CA: Critical Thinking Press and Software (www. criticalthinking.com). (ERIC Document Reproduction Service No. ED 404 836; microfiche only).

O'Donnell, A. M. (1999) Structuring dyadic interaction through scripted cooperation. In A. M. O'Donnell and A. King (eds.), *Cognitive Perspectives on Peer Learning.* Mahwah, NJ: Erlbaum.

O'Donnell, A. M. and Topping, K. (1998) Peers assessing peers: possibilities and problems. In K. Topping and S. Ehly (eds.), *Peer-Assisted Learning.* Mahwah, NJ: Erlbaum.

Overett, J. and Donald, D. (1998) Paired Reading: effects of a parent involvement programme in a disadvantaged community in South Africa. *British Journal of Educational Psychology*, 68, 347–56.

Oxley, L. and Topping, K. (1990) Peer-tutored Cued Spelling with seven- to nine-year-olds. *British Educational Research Journal*, 16 (1), 63–78.

Palincsar, A. S. and Brown, A. L. (1988) Teaching and practicing thinking skills to promote comprehension in the context of group problem-solving. *Remedial and Special Education (RASE)*, 9 (1), 53–9.

Paratore, J. R. and McCormack, R. L. (1997) *Peer Talk in the Classroom*. Newark, DE: International Reading Association.

Paris, S. G. (1991) Assessment and remediation of metacognitive aspects of reading comprehension. *Topics in Language Disorders*, 12, 32–50.

Perkins, D. N. and Grotzer, T. A. (1997) Teaching intelligence. *American Psychologist*, 52 (10), 1125–53.

Pickens, J. and McNaughton, S. (1988) Peer tutoring of comprehension strategies. *Educational Psychology*, 8 (1), 67–80.

Postlethwaite, T. N. and Ross, K. N. (1992) *Effective Schools in Reading: Implications for Educational Planners*. The Hague: International Association for the Evaluation of Educational Achievement.

Powell, S. (1987) Improving critical thinking: a review. *Educational Psychology*, 7 (3), 169–85.

Pressley, M. and Woloshyn, V. E. (eds.) (1995) *Cognitive Strategy Instruction that Really Improves Children's Academic Performance*. (2nd ed.). Cambridge, MA: Brookline Books.

Rand, Y., Mintzker, R., Hoffmann, M. B. and Friedlender, Y. (1981) The Instrumental Enrichment programme: immediate and long-term effects. In P. Mittler (ed.), *Frontiers of Knowledge: Mental Retardation*. Vol. 1. Baltimore: University Park Press.

Raphael, T. E. (1986) Teaching Question Answer Relationships, revisited. *Reading Teacher*, 39 (6), 516–22.

Raths, L. E., Jonas, A., Rothstein, A. and Wasserman, S. (1967) *Teaching for Thinking: Theory and Application*. Columbus, OH: Charles E. Merrill.

Redding, R. E. (1990) Metacognitive instruction: trainers teach thinking skills. *Performance Improvement Quarterly*, 3 (1), 27–41.

Rosenberg V. (1989) *Reading, Writing and Thinking: Critical Connections*. New York: McGraw-Hill.

Rosenshine, B. and Meister, C. (1994) Reciprocal teaching: a review of the research. *Review of Educational Research*, 64 (4), 479–530.

Rosenshine, B., Meister, C. and Chapman, S. (1996) Teaching students to generate questions: a review of intervention studies. *Review of Educational Research*, 66 (2), 181–221.

Ross, J. D. and Ross, C. M. (1976) *Ross Test of Higher Cognitive Processes*. Novato, CA: Academic Therapy Publications (www.atpub.com).

Royer, J. M. (1993) Techniques and procedures for assessing cognitive skills. *Review of Educational Research*, 63 (2), 201–43.

Saunders, W. M. (1989) Collaborative writing tasks and peer interaction. *International Journal of Educational Research*, 13 (1), 101–12.

Savell, J. M., Twohig, P. T. and Rachford, D. L. (1986) Empirical status of Feuerstein's Instrumental Enrichment technique as a method of teaching thinking skills. *Review of Educational Research*, 56 (4), 381–409.

Scardamalia, M. and Bereiter, C. (1986) Research on written composition. In M. C. Wittrock (ed.), *Handbook of Research on Teaching* (3rd ed.). New York: Macmillan.

Scardamalia, M., Bereiter, C., and Goelman, H. (1982). The role of production factors in writing ability. In M. Nystrand (ed.), *What Writers Know: The Language, Process and Structure of Written Discourse*. New York: Academic Press.

Schulz, K. (1997) Do you want to be in my story? Collaborative writing in an urban primary classroom. *Journal of Literacy Research*, 29 (2), 253–88.

Scoble, J. (1988) Cued Spelling in adult literacy: a case study. *Paired Reading Bulletin*, 4, 93–6.

Scoble, J. (1989) Cued Spelling and Paired Reading in adult basic education in Ryedale. *Paired Learning*, 5, 57–62.

Scoble, J., Topping, K. and Wigglesworth, C. (1988) Training family and friends as adult literacy tutors. *Journal of Reading*, 31 (5), 410–17.

Scottish Office Education Department (1991) *Curriculum and Assessment in Scotland: National Guidelines English Language 5–14*. Edinburgh: Scottish Office Education Department.

Shayer, M. and Beasley, F. (1987) Does Instrumental Enrichment work? *British Educational Research Journal*, 13, 101–19.

Simmons, D., Fuchs, D., Fuchs, L. S., Pate, J. and Mathes, P. (1994) Importance of instructional complexity and role reciprocity to class-wide peer tutoring. *Learning Disabilities Research and Practice*, 9, 203–12.

Sindelar, P. T. (1982) The effects of cross-aged tutoring on the comprehension skills of remedial reading students. *Journal of Special Education*, 16 (2), 199–206.

Smith, D. and Johnson, D. (1995) The efficacy of Paired Reading in South African primary schools. In D. Johnson (ed.), *Educational Management and Policy: Research, Theory and Practice in South Africa*. Bristol: Centre for International Studies in Education, School of Education, University of Bristol. (ERIC Document Reproduction Service No. ED 383 070).

Stenmark, J. K., Thompson, V. and Cossey, R. (1986) *Family Math*. Equals: Lawrence Hall of Science, Berkeley, CA:

Stiggins, R. J., Griswold, M. M. and Wikelund, K. R. (1989) Measuring thinking skills through classroom assessment. *Journal of Educational Measurement*, 26 (3), 233–46.

Sutherland, J. A. and Topping, K. J. (1999) Collaborative creative writing in eight year olds: comparing cross ability fixed role and same ability reciprocal role pairing. *Journal of Research in Reading*, 22 (2), 154–79.

Teddlie, C. and Reynolds, D. (eds.) (1999) *The International Handbook of School Effectiveness Research*. London: Taylor & Francis.

Tizard, J., Schofield, W. N. and Hewison, J. (1982) Collaboration between teachers and parents in assisting children's reading. *British Journal of Educational Psychology*, 52, 1–15.

Toomey, D. (1991) Parents hearing reading: Lessons for school practice from the British and Australasian research. Paper presented at the annual meeting of the American Educational Research Association, Chicago, April 3–7. (ERIC Document Reproduction Service No. ED 333 355).

Toomey, D. (1993) Parents hearing their children read: a review. *Educational Research*, 35 (3), 223–36.

Topping, K. J. (1992a) Short- and long-term follow-up of parental involvement in reading projects. *British Educational Research Journal*, 18 (4), 369–79.

Topping, K. J. (1992b) The effectiveness of paired reading in ethnic minority homes. *Multicultural Teaching*, 10 (2), 19–23.

Topping, K. J. (1995a) *Paired Reading, Spelling and Writing: The Handbook for Teachers and Parents*. London: Cassell.

Topping, K. J. (1995b) Effective tutoring systems for family literacy. *Reading and Writing Quarterly*, 11 (3), 285–95.

Topping, K. J. (1995c) Achieving more with less: Raising reading standards. In C. Gains and D. Wray (eds.), *Reading: Issues and Directions*. Stafford: National Association for Special Educational Needs and United Kingdom Reading Association.

Topping, K. J. (1995d) Cued Spelling: a powerful technique for parent and peer tutoring. *Reading Teacher*, 48 (5), 374–83. (also in the Society for Developmental Education (ed.), *Teaching for Success: Strengthening Child-centred Classrooms*. Resource Book. 8th ed. Peterborough, NH: Crystal Springs Books.

Topping, K. J. (1996) The effectiveness of family literacy. In S. W. Wolfendale and K. J. Topping (eds.), *Family Involvement in Literacy: Effective Partnerships in Education*. London: Cassell.

Topping, K. J. (1997a) Family electronic literacy: home–school links through computers. *Reading (UKRA)*, 31 (2), 12–21.

Topping, K. J. (1997b) Process and outcome in paired reading: a reply to Winter. *Educational Psychology in Practice*, 13 (2), 75–86.

Topping, K. J. (1998a) Effective tutoring in America Reads: a reply to Wasik. *Reading Teacher*, 52 (1), 42–50.

Topping, K. J. (1998b) *The Paired Science Handbook: Parental Involvement and Peer Tutoring in Science*. London: Fulton.

Topping, K. J. (2000b) *Tutoring by Peers, Family and Volunteers*. Geneva: International Bureau of Education, UNESCO. Also [on-line]: www.ibe.unesco.org/Publications/Practice/practice.htm. (Also in translation in Chinese and Spanish.)

Topping, K. J. (2001a) *Peer Assisted Learning: A Practical Guide for Teachers*. Cambridge, MA: Brookline Books.

Topping, K. J. (2001b) Paired reading with peers and parents: factors in effectiveness and new developments. In C. Harrison and M. Coles (eds.), *The Reading for Real Handbook*, 2nd ed. London: Routledge (in press).

Topping, K. J. and Bamford, J. (1998a) *Parental Involvement and Peer Tutoring in Mathematics and Science: Developing Paired Maths into Paired Science*. London: Fulton.

Topping, K. J. and Bamford, J. (1998b) *The Paired Maths Handbook: Parental Involvement and Peer Tutoring in Mathematics*. London: Fulton.

Topping, K. J. and Bryce, A. Cross-age peer tutoring of reading and thinking in the primary school: a controlled study of influence on thinking skills. Paper submitted for publication.

Topping, K. J. and Ehly, S. (eds.) (1998) *Peer Assisted Learning*. Mahwah, NJ: Erlbaum.

Topping, K. J. and Lindsay, G. A. (1992a) The structure and development of the Paired Reading technique. *Journal of Research in Reading*, 15 (2), 120–36.

Topping, K. J. and Lindsay, G. A. (1992b) Paired Reading: a review of the literature. *Research Papers in Education*, 7 (3), 199–246.

Topping, K. J. and Lindsay, G. A. (1992c) Parental involvement in reading: the influence of socio-economic status and supportive home visiting. *Children and Society*, 5 (4), 306–16.

Topping, K. J. and Paul, T. D. (1999) Computer-assisted assessment of practice at reading: a large scale survey using Accelerated Reader data. *Reading and Writing Quarterly*, 15 (3), 213–31.

Topping, K. J. and Whiteley, M. (1990) Participant evaluation of parent-tutored and peer-tutored projects in reading. *Educational Research*, 32 (1), 14–32.

Topping, K. J. and Whiteley, M. (1993) Sex differences in the effectiveness of peer tutoring. *School Psychology International*, 14 (1), 57–67.

Topping, K. J. and Wolfendale, S. W. (1995) The effectiveness of family literacy programmes. *Reading (UKRA)*, 29 (3), 26–33.

Topping, K. J., Nixon, J., Sutherland, J. and Yarrow, F. (2000) Paired writing: a framework for effective collaboration. *Reading (UKRA)*, 34 (2), 79–89.

Topping, K. J., Shaw, M. C. and Bircham, A.M. (1997) Family electronic literacy: home-school links through audiotaped books. *Reading (UKRA)*, 31 (2), 7–11.

Van Kraayenoord, C. E. and Paris, S. G. (1997) Australian students' self-appraisal of their work samples and academic progress. *Elementary School Journal*, 97 (5), 523–37.

Voss, J. F., Wiley, J. and Carretero, M. (1995) Acquiring intellectual skills. *Annual Review of Psychology*, 46, 155–81.

Watt, J. M. and Topping, K. J. (1993) Cued Spelling: a comparative study of parent and peer tutoring. *Educational Psychology in Practice*, 9 (2), 95–103.

Winter, S. (1996) Paired Reading: three questions. *Educational Psychology in Practice*, 12 (3), 33–41.

Wolfendale, S. W. and Topping, K. J. (eds.) (1996) *Family Involvement in Literacy: Effective Partnerships in Education*. London: Cassell.

Yarrow, F. and Topping, K. J. (2001) Collaborative writing: the effects of metacognitive prompting and structured peer interaction. *British Journal of Educational Psychology*, 71 (2), 261–82.

Yuill, N. and Oakhill, J. (1988) Effects of inference awareness training on poor reading comprehension. *Applied Cognitive Psychology*, 2, 33–45.

Author Index

For works with multiple authors, only the first author is indexed.

Subject Index